COMMON LAW AND SHARIA IN NIGERIA:

AN UNRESOLVED PROBLEM OF COEXISTENCE

B.A.T BALEWA, mni.

First Published 2002 by
FOURTH DIMENSION PUBLISHING CO., LTD.
16 Fifth Ave. City Layout, P.M.B. 01164. Enugu. Nigeria email:
info@fdpbooks.com fdpbooks@aol.com,
Web site: http://www.fdpbooks.com.

ISBN 978-156-514-4

Design and Typesetting by
Fourth Dimension Publishers, Enugu

Dedication

This book is dedicated to the Honourable Justice Taslirn Oluwole Elias, a pioneer in the development of African legal thought. His main area of concern is the basis of law and loyalty in society. Behind much of his thinking lie a fruitful combination of experience and ideas which can nourish the thinking of and inspire the African elite in their search for the link between law, religion and politics in a given society.

TABLE OF CONTENTS

PREFACE

The Sharia controversy has been with us for over ten years now. Two strong viewpoints have formed the basis of this controversy. There are those who believe that Sharia, because of its religious content, should not be reflected in the Nigerian Constitution. The other side believe that Sharia, as a fully fledged legal system, should have a definite place in the Constitution. Nigerians genuinely interested in the peaceful development of their country must be asking themselves self-searching questions about this stubborn issue. When is the controversy going to be resolved? What are some of the possible consequences of delaying action in finding practical solutions to the problem? The fact that the Federal Government has intervened by stopping debate on the subject in the Constituent Assembly offers only temporary relief. The wisdom of the decision taken by the Government is being questioned. Whichever viewpoint finally prevails of the two, one side in the argument is bound to feel aggrieved. Isn't there another way out of this impasse? These are the questions that agitated my mind throughout the deliberations of the Constituent Assembly on this issue.

An excellent way to begin to identify a possible way out is for each side in a controversy to ensure that it has a good grasp of the inward significance of the motives and actions of the other. The more the two sides understand each other, the more sympathetic and objective they shall be when the time comes to receive the final verdict. It is for this reason that this little booklet has been prepared. It is hoped that the reader will find that it covers practically all of the pertinent arguments on each side. The advantage to be gained by having the opportunity to understand something of the other side's points of view on important matters is imperative for people who live together. This importance is self-evident, especially in matters of religion, which are by their very nature sensitive.

The philosophy of law and jurisprudence attempts to find answers to problems of human relationships in the course of ordinary daily transactions in organized society. Law covers a wide range of human activity, but it is clearly distinguishable from the value judgments it implements. Professor E. H. Levi observes that the problems of law centre around the source and limit of the coercive power of state which is brought to bear on the administration of justice in a community. The human relationships which law determines, though legal in nature, are often taken for granted. This is clearly so in societies which share common basic values. During times of social distress or political instability, when the need to appeal to higher law arises, the distinction between law and value judgement often has the tendency to become blurred. Inherent in these problems is the prescriptive motivation to want to define what some aspects of law should or ought to be, according to one set of perceptions or another. The cases of *United States vs Holmes* (decided in 1842) and in England, the *Queen vs Dudley and Stephens* (decided in 1884) have often been cited as classical examples of extreme situations which raise intriguing questions of philosophy and jurisprudence. In each case, innocent people were killed in an extremely complicated set of circumstances. The question raised before the courts in each of the countries concerned was whether or not the killings were justified in the context of the respective circumstances in which they occurred. Nigeria is today faced with a similar philosophical question. Her problem found expression in the inability of two separate constituent Assemblies (1978 and 1988) to distinguish between the concept of law and that of value judgment.

Members of both assemblies failed to recognize the need to distinguish between the question of constitutionality i.e. formal power to promulgate from the wisdom of legislation, on the one hand, and legislative and judicial justice on the other. The issue before each body was whether or not a particular legal system, which operates in the society, ought to be reflected in the country's constitution and, if so, the level at which it should do so in the judicial hierarchy.

Central to the problem that was put before the two Constituent Assemblies are the very delicate nature of modern democratic institutions and the nature of law itself. Within the systems operated by advanced democracies, which Nigeria tries hard to emulate, the dialogue on the nature of law is still going on. Law in these countries is not regarded as static or merely customary. To them, the legislature is there to change the law in order to enhance progress. This change in law is not without far reaching implications for their societies. Montaigue warned in his essay entitled "Of Custom, and That we should Not Change Law Received", that:

> The legislator of the Thurians ordained that whoever would go about either to abolish an old law, or establish a new one should present himself with a halter about his neck to the people to end, that if the innovation he would introduce should not be approved by everyone, he might immediately be hanged (Vol. 25, p. 48c)

The reservation people have about a change in law stems from the fact that any change in law raises the philosophical question of whether the law is always improved when it is changed. St Aquinas expressed the same concern when he asked what the purpose of human law is and what its function is. In his attempts to answer these vital questions he argued that since divine law directs man to his eternal beatitude and natural law to his happiness on this earth, then human positive law is needed only to lead man to virtue. He concluded that while there is in man a natural aptitude for virtue, this does not mean that all men are necessarily virtuous in all or even most of their actions.

The problem facing the nations which aspire to become

democratic is three-fold. Firstly, at what stage are they going to enter the controversy over the different paths to the rule of law? Secondly, in a multi-religious society where basic values differ widely, how are the differences over the nature of law going to be reconciled? Thirdly, to what extent can one type of legal system predominate over others within the context of the same society without the entire society becoming destabilized? The importance of the issues involved in the evolution of acceptable legal systems in these young countries obviates the need to find answers to these questions.

It seems logical to suggest that, in times of difficulties or political and social instability, amongst the most urgent needs in countries which desire to be democratic is the crucial one of the full understanding of the basic philosophies of law and jurisprudence. The next most important requirements then becomes the practical application of these philosophies to the fundamental realities of each respective society, using the understanding as a framework. This obviates the need for careful consideration of the different concepts of law and how best they can be used to aid the attainment of an all embracing and universally acceptable legal system. This, far more than anything else, offers the best hope for enhancing political stability and the protection of the best of a nation's heritage during the uncertain struggle for development in today's turbulent and ever-changing world.

A parallel issue which should be of immense interest to us is the careful manner in which the British and the French planned their approach to the tackling of their problem of governing us Africans. If it was in their interest to study the social institutions of the people they colonized in order to govern them peacefully, it surely behooves us also to study our own different social and religious institutions in order to enhance our peaceful development. It is the move towards the realization of this simple and yet complex objective that this booklet seeks to promote.

The work began as an article entitled "Common Law and Sharia in Nigeria" which appeared in the Sunday New Nigerian of 29th January, 1989. The interest the article generated led many friends, both Christians and Muslims who read it, to encourage me to develop it for further publication. It is believed such a work may be useful both for students interested in comparative studies and for the general reader who wishes to broaden his knowledge of the sources of our legal forms and their implications for the future development of our national legal system. I am particularly indebted to Hon. Justice Muhammad Buba Ardo, Deputy Chairman of the Constituent Assembly, Alhaji Ahmed Joda, Professor D. A. Ijalaiye, Dr Hassan Lawal of the University of Jos and Alhaji Muhammad A. Wabili and Dr N. M. Adeyemi of the National Institute for Policy and Strategic Studies, Kuru, each of whom read the original manuscript and offered constructive criticisms and useful advice which I found most invaluable in the preparation of this booklet. Last, but not the least, I must express my profound gratitude to Ben Okareme who typed the manuscript with great care and competence. I thank all for the encouragement and I hope the work will achieve the desired objective.

It is important to stress the point that the ideas expressed in this work are mine, and that I alone am therefore responsible for any errors or shortcomings to be found in it. I tried as hard as is humanly possible to be objective in my treatment of all the relevant subject matters in the firm belief that objectivity promotes understanding.

B. A. T. Balewa
30th April 1989

INTRODUCTION

For the second time in 10 years, the Federal Government has had to intercede in an ongoing debate on Sharia in the Constituent Assembly. The first time was in 1978 when General Olusegun Obasanjo, the then Head of State, had to intervene to abate the heated controversy over Sharia. That history often repeats itself is a well known truism. However, for it to have done so quickly and so completely with no apparent lesson learnt is a very sad reflection on our society and its development. This sequence of events would appear to question our competence as a people to resolve internal differences without recourse to antagonism and conflict. The imbroglio is ostensibly a religious one, but its political nature becomes all too evident on closer analysis. Members of the Constituent Assembly and indeed the Nigerian public at large must now begin to reflect seriously on what the actual reasons behind this repeated friction were and are. The respective Federal Governments must have had good cause for each of the acts of intervention on this issue. When responsible people, such as members of the Constituent Assembly, forsake their own individual private conscience for the sake of an unproductive exercise in fanciful circumlocution on religion, politics or metaphysics, they are in effect leading their nation along the shortest route to chaos. This seems to explain the cause of the Federal Government's action regarding the Sharia controversy on both occasions mentioned.

Most would agree that a Constitution is supposed to be a forward looking legal document designed both to alleviate and to guard against society's repeatable, existing and foreseeable development problems. Implicit in the very nature of the preparation of a Constitution is the obvious need for coherent assessment, special attention to detail and well reasoned deduction, all tempered with an element of justice and fair play. In the words of a highly respected philosopher: "...a Constitution is legitimate only when each law is a dictate of reason" (J. Adler and P. Wolff in *Philosophy of Law and Jurisprudence*, pp. 73-100). However, as regards the discussions on some aspects of the proposed Nigerian Constitution, many people are now reaching the conclusion that the bulk of the argument being presented regarding the inclusion or non-inclusion of Sharia in the Constitution have been based more on emotion than on reason.

CHAPTER 1

LAW AND RELIGION IN A SOCIETY

Before we proceed to discuss the validity or otherwise of the arguments against Sharia, it would facilitate our understanding to have a deeper understanding of the function of a legal system in any society. A legal system is the foundation upon which social relations are set for the purpose of the *common good* in a society. It is for this very reason that, from the instant that man became a social animal, the law has been relied upon to set out the terms of his co- existence with his fellow man. This ought to be the way in which Christians and Muslims in Nigeria should view their legal systems and the laws that are to govern their cc- existence.

Arguments among academics on what exactly the function of religion is have been going on for centuries. Some have argued that belief in it regulates social affairs in this world and distribute rewards and punishments in the next. Others see religion as the most powerful motive in human history. Still others see it purely as a mere device designed to make "the injustices of existing social order tolerable to those who suffer it". It is for this reason that religion and politics can never be separated in the minds of either those who believe in them or those who seek to govern them. It cannot be denied that religious conceptions have influenced most of mankind's concepts and institutions of government; law, sovereignty, social welfare, education and political obligation. This is particularly so in the concepts of modern government in the West. The same, of course, applies to the concept of government in Islamic societies.

We need to stop for a while to reflect deeply on why the early Christian and Muslim theologians were and are still interested in law and politics. Is there any relationship between these topics and religion? The answers to these questions are to be found in Hobbes's theories of morals, politics and obligation. Hobbes' enquiry into human behaviour is based on the assumption that the task of political philosophy is to discover how to maintain a stable ordered society and how to avoid disorder in handling its affairs. According to him, the natural state of mankind is a state of war, where every man is enemy to every man." This naturally leads to a perpetual fear and danger to life. The question theologians/philosophers sought to answer is, whether this state of anarchy, into which mankind tends to drift, is to be left to take its natural course. Hobbes convinced himself that the cause of this desirable human behaviour lies in man's inherent nature - the desire for self-preservation, manifesting itself in greed, acquisitiveness and competition. Indeed, these are the selfsame characteristics that we clearly recognize and so readily accept in animals but strive to suppress in ourselves, thereby creating a distinction in the motivating factors that guide "human" as set aside from "animal" behaviour in nature. The tendency is to conveniently forget that we, too, are animals. Sophisticated, intelligent and superior, but glorified animals nonetheless, we, too, are ordinarily subject to the dictates of nature.

Political philosophers have pointed out that the desire for self-preservation gives rise to a desire for pleasure. Pleasure in this sense is the appearance in consciousness of what is conducive to life. It follows that man's desire to end the natural state of war (continued preservation) necessarily leads him to desire peace for continued life in the future. It is not difficult therefore to see that this desire for peace finds expression in law, politics and morals. Hobbes's theory of obligation and his political theories lay emphasis on the significance of a distinction between what is natural and what is artificial. He concludes that what we see all around us is nature or the natural and what we make ourselves is art or artificial. Hobbes points out that to us, the world is natural but to God it is artificial because he treated it.

A rational man who seeks a state of peace in order to preserve his life, is said to respond to the laws of nature. Emmanuel Kant, the German philosopher, sees the fundamental laws of nature as hypothetical imperatives which prescribe a means to our interest. In his work, *The Science of Right*, he developed a theory of natural right of a natural law. He speaks of natural right as the right which is based upon pure rational principles which are discoverable by reason. To him, it is the right which belongs to every one by nature independent of any judicial experience. It is important to note that the key word here is "principles". Like St Aquinas, Kant does not deal with all laws in their complexity, but only with their principles. Montesquieu's, *The Spirit of Laws*, dwells more on the circumstances which affect laws. Law, to him, is human reason. Since peoples differ, he suggests that their laws should be adopted in such a manner to suit the people for whom they are made. Rousseau's description of law is very much like Hobbes' natural obligation. In his view, it is the will of the people that makes law. He argues:

> when the whole people decrees for the whole people, it is considering only itself; and if a relation is then formed, it is between two aspects of the entire object, without there being any division of the whole. In that case, the matter about which the decree is made is, like the decreeing will, general. This act is what I called law. (p.399d)

Rousseau's emphasis on "collective will" which in his view is what makes law, is very relevant to the Nigerian situation. The problem we have today is the paucity of that collective will, or the elements that make it strong enough to make law. Rousseau's conclusion of his discourse on law is even more relevant to our situation. He concludes:

> On this view, we at once see that it can no longer be asked whose business it is to make laws, since they are acts of the general will; nor whether the prince (read ruler) is above the law since he is a member of the State; nor whether the law can be unjust, since no one is unjust to himself; nor how we can be both free and subject to the laws, since they are but registers of our wills (pp. 399-400a)

We are told that the general will is general in two senses. First, it must be directed to general aims, and second, it must be the will of the whole people! As far as the Nigerian legal system is concerned, our will, if any, seem to be directed toward conflicting aims. It follows that we have not arrived at a situation whereby we can mobilize the will of the whole people. This is the crux of our problem. It is the habits of compliance in society which helps create the general will and these habits are reinforced by the probability of enforcement of the law against those who may transgress it. This is how people decide their fate. Thus, without these compliance habits, the future of a society is surrounded by uncertainty, like a quagmire stubbornly hindering all attempts at progress.

In his book, *Leviathan*, Hobbes opines that the words "law" applies only to a command issued by someone who has the right to be obeyed. This receipt of reason must have led the early Christian and Muslim theologians to conclude that laws should be regarded as commands issued to us by God who has to the right to be obey. This is what makes laws hypothetical imperatives which tell us what we ought to do if we are to preserve our lives, this tendency inhuman beings to want to service, is what Hobbies describes in his book, *de Give*, as "natural obligation".

This brings us neatly to the point where we should ask why the source of both Christian and Islamic laws is to be found in their respective Sacred Books. The adherents of both faiths believe firmly that their laws emanate from the God they worship. Even a cursory study of the two religions reveals that they are, worshipping the same God. The only practical and significant difference being the distinct socio-cultural settings on which each faith historically rests. Other differences are evident which, in reality, are only minor differences of detail, but these deserve special treatment in their own right and are therefore outside the scope of this analysis. The salient point here is that, according to all qualified historical sources, both Christians and Muslims, each in their own different way, worship the same God. Therefore, if the God is the same, and the ideals are the same, then why should there by any differences in these two set of laws? From all indications the difference appears to be man made. The orthodox view of both faiths is that man achieves fulfillment in affirming and carrying out the divine to question commands. Most early classical theologians believed that it is always wrong to question the divine commands, but obversely, Pometheans believe men must resist them relentlessly. Why should we resists divine commands? The only logical explanation we can offer is that either because we find them inconvenient to obey or we do not understand them. Imam Rashid Husain cites a classic example if the type of inconvenience which is occasioned by selfish motives, he argues:

> An assumption of one race of its superiority over other has condemned millions of human lives to their deaths and has now through the banner of so-called civilization, science and high technology created the super-powers rivalry with an advance notice to each other of an impending total extinction of human race on this planet.

In order to perpetuate the supremacy of one race over the others through man-made catastrophes, certain sections of mankind deemed it fit ~develop strange and diverse ideologies and other ill-conceived political devices. It will be recalled that the idea of race superiority emanates from the theory that racial differences denote natural inequality among races. Count Arthur de Gobintau, a French contemporary of Karl Marx propounded the theory. The idea gained ground rapidly in Europe and is believed to have motivated John Stuart Mill's *Essay on Liberty*, Marx's, *Critique of Political Economy* and Charles Darwin's *Origins of Species*. The theory was given a boost by the Gobineau Club founded by Wagner, a German, and Houston Stewart Chamberlain (1855-1926), a renegade Englishman.

Chamberlain's book on the racial theory, *The Foundations of the Nineteenth Century*, which came out in 1899 encouraged the English, the French and the Germans to dominate much of what is today described as the third world. The basic idea of racial inequality rests on the questionable belief that racial differences or divisions of mankind are inescapable and fundamental. In his contribution of *European Political Ideas*, David Thompson observes that this theory is based on the belief that the outward differences of colour, hair and nose reflect the emotional and mental aptitudes of mankind. The theory attributed to the Aryans (white race) an outstanding vigour and inventiveness, the Mongul (yellow race) mediocrity and impassivity which is said to be responsible for their law abidingness and stable character. The Negroid (black race) is credited with outstanding musical and artistic virtues. The implications of this theory for mankind is that the Aryan initiatives are responsible for the great civilization of the world. History now disproves this theory. We all know that the great civilizations began in Asia and Africa and spread to Europe where the refining processes continued.

Indeed, not all the Aryans believed in the theory of racial superiority but experience has shown that the few influential elite who believed in it had attempted to establish and perpetuate its dominance. The slave trade, colonialism in Asia and Africa, the attempt to exterminate the Jews, segregation in America, the nuclear bombing of Japan rather than Germany (the originator of the war), apartheid in South Africa and the intractable North-South dialogue in the United Nations are different manifestations of the effect of Gobineau's theory of racial superiority. A pertinent question that should agitate our minds is whether or not the theory is dead. Political theorists are agreed that in spite of the advanced civilization the work has attained, the theory is very much alive. In his conclusion in~ the book, Political Ideas David Thompson observes:

> in the context of these recurring tendencies racialist theories may then be seen as a modem counterpart or variant of those principles of exclusion, intolerance, absolutism and claims to elitism which have been persistent throughout the experience of European civilization. The ecclesiastic who claim priority in salvation for his co-religionists, the nationalist who exalts his own nation's manifest destiny, the Marxist who claims moral superiority and historically inevitable victory for the proletariat, are on this view not intrinsically different from the fanatical adherent of creeds of racial superiority (Political Ideas - pp. 195-196).

If Machiavelli's political theory is still valid as a defence of a form of political activity motivated by "reason d'etat" at all cost, then the possibility of continuance of the theory cannot be hastily discarded. The seemingly radical ideas culminating in the concept of welfare state designed to appease the unfortunate in advanced societies and foreign aid to redress injustice to the victims of the theory of race superiority are not enough to curb the excesses of the theory.

The purpose of this fairly long digression is to stress the seriousness of the dangers of deviation from the principles of natural law and social justice as enunciated by the Holy Books and early great Christian and Islamic theologians. The emphasis of the early theologians is on "justice". Actions were seen in terms of whether they are just or not. By implication, the more we deviate from those basic principles the more we create a situation which induces society to express periodic moral outbursts at what it sees as particularly inhuman and degrading view of life. Regrettably the only solution proffered is more sophisticated political control. Moral and normative control are yet to attract the attention of modern political thinkers. The obvious consequence of this trend is the declining importance of law as a normative control of human passion.

Today, the incalculable cost of maintaining racial dominance is unbelievable. Imam Husain points out that:

> The economic cost of maintaining the dominant position (of Superpowers) is estimated to be $1 trillion a year which is the equivalent of $2 million a minute. It is reckoned that a fifth of that expenditure alone is sufficient to eliminate hunger in the world by the year 2000. Regrettably, because this is not convenient, this is unlikely to happen.

A view expressed by St. Augustine seems to support this contention. In his work, *Against the Academics*, he interpreted the biblical doctrine of creation (the first five words of Genesis). In his interpretation, he constructed an amazing synthesis which Mortimer J. Adler and Seymour Cain in their book, *Religion and Theology*, described as two irreconcilable views. He argues:

> After many centuries and many disputes, at length a system of philosophy was discovered which in my opinion is most true. It is not what our sacred religion so rightly abhors, a philosophy of the material world, but reveals another and intelligible world.

Indeed every thinker is subject to different interpretations. This is because he presents familiar facts in a novel perspective and arranges them in unfamiliar fashion. The philosopher, for example, is not free from ambiguity since he too would have difficulty in adjusting his ideas in an unfamiliar field. It is generally agreed that in such delicate areas of thought as morals and law, which have direct links with religion, many differences of interpretation are likely to arise. For example, differences in the meaning St. Augustine attaches to the doctrine of creation, have persisted to this day. These differences exist also in the work of other religious philosophers and their interpretation of God's divine injunctions. For example, in the name of modernization Egypt and Tunisia reformed the Sharia Courts and secularized their legal systems in *1955* and *1956* respectively. Instead, Islamic personal law based on Sharia is now administered by a unified system at national courts with civil and criminal jurisdiction. The greatest departure from Sharia is to be found in the Turkish and Albanian legal systems where both civil and criminal laws are secularized. Arguments among scholars continue to rage on whether or not this version of Islam is different from that of Muslims elsewhere. The real issue is whether or not any deviations from the established principles' of law is tantamount to a violation of God's injunctions and therefore a change in peoples faith. This has been the source of endless debate.

History tells us that in some Islamic states, whenever a ruler appears to have deviated from Sharia in the system of their governance, reaction from scholars have always occurred. For example, under Emperor Akbar's successors, Jehanghir and Shah Jehan there were reactions which culminated in the complete reversal of Akbar's policy under Aurungzib in *AD 1656*. As a result of similar reactions Pakistan has completed her plans to return to Sharia. It will be recalled that Islamic law was reformed during the British administration of India of which Pakistan was formerly a part.

The question that will continue to preoccupy the minds of thinkers in law and religion is the extent to which reforms of any legal system can go without the risk of some deviation from the true meaning of the divine injunctions that form their foundations. The problem we have to live with is the limitation on our ability to arrive at an exact definition of the concept of the term, "divine injunction".

Our discussion would then lead us to the conclusion that theologians and political philosophers are interested in law because of its salutary effect on human being in mankind's effort to find peace and progress. Another conclusion we can safely draw is that law is more likely to be obeyed if it is seen as a command from God and because of its capacity to help us preserve our lives. By implication, law is designed to help us save ourselves from ourselves.

Whenever there exists a multi-religious society, there must also exist an array of devices which serve to provide and perpetuate a climate of peaceful and cooperative co-existence in both the interaction of people and in the administration of justice in their society. These are some of the crucial preconditions for a progressive, stable and harmonious society, and above all, for better understanding amongst the adherents of different religious faiths. It is in this respect that the idea of having a High Court, a Customary Court of Appeal and a Federal Sharia Court of Appeal in Nigerian legal system calls for some deep and sober reflection. Under such an amalgam of systems the fears of the adherents of all the three broad types of religious faiths are more likely to be allayed and their respective interests accommodated accordingly.

In discussing the future of a multi-religious society like that of Nigeria, some time must be devoted to the accurate definition of the role of "legal systems" within the operational context of the society. Law, we are told, is the authentic will of a people and the practical expression of their desire to be ruled by it. (see law and the Koran: The Koran, translated for the British Foreign Secretary, Lord Carteret by George Sale, pp. 6-96). If it is the will of the millions of Muslims in Nigeria to be ruled by Sharia, then reason ought to dictate that such desire be respected and allowed by all Nigerians. To deny them such a right is to deprive them of one of their fundamental human rights. Such an act would not only be a manifestly unjust one but would also be contrary to the spirit of the Nigerian Constitution. Yet, the Constituent Assembly has been constituted to frame an acceptable Constitution. This can only be done by laying the foundation of justice on behalf of all Nigerians irrespective of their faiths.

CHAPTER 2

THE CASE AGAINST SHARIA

Among the most significant and recurrent contentions raised against Sharia are as follows:

(a) Sharia is a purely religious legal system comprising a set of divine injunctions which applies to Muslims only and plays the same role in Islam as Canon Law does in Christianity;
(b) to include Sharia in the Constitution is to pave the way for the islamization of the Nigerian state;
(c) inclusion of a purely religious legal system in the Constitution affects Nigeria's secular status;
(d) the Common Law which operates in Nigeria is not a Christian law; and
(e) the compulsory trial of Non-Muslims in Sharia Courts.

The genesis of the Sharia controversy is to be found in the idea that Nigeria is a secular state. The crux of the argument before the Constituent Assembly is that, since Nigeria is a secular state, her constitution should not reflect any religious undertones. The argument further suggests that because of the perceived religious character of Sharia, it should neither be entrenched in the Constitution nor should its operation be financed from public funds. This line of argument raises two pertinent questions. Is Nigeria really a secular state? If it turns out that is not, what is lost? Answers to these questions are to be found in our own different perceptions of the concept of a secular state and the advantages that secularity offers to a society. These matters shall be dealt with in due course.

Those who espouse the view that the Sharia legal system is merely a body of religious laws, are doing so out of a series of misconceptions and assumptions. Regrettably, this view is a widely believed dictum. The first significant point is that there is no emperical evidence to show that Sharia is not purely a -religious law. A careful analysis of its historical background would reveal that it is a cogent, competent and coherent legal system which has been designed to carry out certain necessary functions within a social system that is operated by Muslims (see Appendix II). The second important point, which follows on from the first, is that every legal system in the history of man has or had the same basis. In other words, there is no legal system in the history of man which is without a religious foundation. The correlation is simple enough. The religions of the world provide the moral codes for the guidance and protection of the individual in society. The legal system of the world do much the same thing, except that they apply to each respective society as a whole. Amongst the beneficiaries of Sharia in the 14th and 15th Century Europe were not only the Muslims but the Christians as well as the Jews. The early Christian scholars were persecuted by the authorities because of their "sacrilegious" academic pursuits and "unholy" scientific discoveries which seemed to threaten conventional beliefs and e often appeared to be in conflict with established Christian IS values. The scholars were protected in Muslim Spain under Sharia which allows freedom of thought in search of knowledge. Similarly, some Jews were able to escape persecution by the authorities who wished to curb the extent of 15 Jewish trade in Europe because of its very real threat to Christian commercial expansionism by taking advantage of the freedom available to them offered under the umbrella of Muslim states and Islamic law and their protection and encouragement of trade -and commerce.

It cannot be denied that, a legal system constitutes the moral of and ethical threads in the fabric of society. It is the embodiment of mores, values, norms and traditions into a coherent set of is rules and regulations which totally and irrefutably govern the interaction of all individuals and groups within an ordered -society. A legal system is, largely, to the society what a set of religious codes is to the individual.

CHAPTER 3

THE SOURCES OF SHARIA

A brief look at the background of Sharia might help to shed some light on how Muslims perceive their religion. First of all, it is important to know that the primary source of Sharia is the Holy Qur'an, that its secondary sources are the Hadith and Sunnah (the teachings of the Prophet Mohammed) and that its tertiary sources are derived from a combination of the following:

(a) Al-Ijma (Consensus of opinion of jurists)
(b) Al-Qiyas (Analogical deductions)
(c) Al-Ijtihad (Research)
(d) Istislah (Public interest)
(e) Istihbab (Prescriptive Legislation)
(f) Saad Al-Dhrai (Preventive legislation) - (See Sharia/Common and Customary Law Courts by Msgr H. Adigwe (1988. pp, 39-40).

Secondly, it is equally important to know that the founders of the four schools of thought in Islam which are connected with the development of concept of Sharia are the renowned Imams (Abu Hanifah, Malik Bin Anas, Mohammed Idris-A1-Shafi'i and Ahmad Mohammed Bin Hanbal) who strove to develop the theory and practice of Sharia over a period of a century and a half beginning from the late 7th Century (AD).

The four orthodox Sunni schools which survive in Islam to this day are identified with views of their founders.

1. **Imam Abu Hanifah (80 - 150 AH (696 - 766 AD)**

Imam Abu Hanifah was born in Kufah (present day Iraq) and his school of thought had profound influence throughout the Turkish Empire, in Northern India, Central Asia and Southern Russia. He was a philosopher deeply versed in Islamic thought. The Hadiya/z is the best known work of this school; it was compiled in about 1196 AD. Research has indicated that no definite work has been attributed to Imam Abu Hanifah himself. However, as a pioneer in the field of Islamic Law, he has a remarkable influence on legal thought in the Muslim world from the 8th Century to the present day.

2. **Imam Malik Bin Anas (93 - 179 AH (709 - 795 AD))**
   Imam Malik, a Yemenese in origin, was born in Medina (Saudi Arabia) shortly after the close of the era of the Tabiun (the companions of Prophet Mohammed) when Medina had become an established centre of higher learning. He was born during the reign of the Ummayyad Caliphate whose territories had expanded up to Europe (Spain), the Maghreb in North Africa and India in Asia. His students were drawn from all these territories to widen their knowledge under his tutelage. He was not only a Muslim theologian with a deep knowledge of the Qur'an, but also placed great emphasis of his scholarship on the Hadith and Sunnah of Prophet Muhammed (see his major work - Al-Muwatta). His main contribution to the development of Islamic Law was the codification of the Medinan Fiqh. His scholarly work has earned him a vivifying influence among jurists in North Africa, India and, to some extent, West Africa.

3. **Imam Muhammad Idris Al-S hafi'i (150 - 204 AH (767 - 820 AD)**
   Al-Shafi'i an eminent scholar and jurist, was born in Gaza on the shores of the Mediterranean Sea. He is described as a unique combination of vision and personal piety fused with literary and philosophic judgement. He belonged to the Quraish tribe and was

therefore a descendant of Prophet Mohammed. He was a student of Imam Malik and was an intellectual of repute. His interest as in the field of Islamic sciences. His scientific approach to Islamic thought made him a controversial figure. He studied and criticized the legal works of the Hanafi and Malik schools. He admired and respected the Muwatta of Imam Malik which, in his-view, was the closest human work to the Holy Qur'an. He served as adviser to the Iraqi Government during the caliphate of Harun-al-Rasheed. His vehement opposition to the doctrine of Mutazilite, which the ruling Caliph supported led him to leave Baghdad for Egypt where he engaged himself in lectures and discourses in the field of law.

Most significant of the contributions made to Islamic jurisprudence by this school of thought is to be found in the work of Ibn Abu Zaid - Kitab al-Risalah Fi-Usul-al-Fiqh. The book, popularly known as al-Risalah, earned Imam Al-Shafi'i the title of the father of Islamic Jurisprudence. He laid great emphasis on the over-riding authority of the Sunnah in his work. He drew heavily on it in formulating the rules of Islamic Law. His followers are to be found in Yeman, Egypt, Syria, East Africa, East Asia (Malaysia, Indonesia) and scattered in other parts of the Muslim world.

4. **Imam Ahmad Bin Muhammad Bin Hanbal (169 - 241 AH (780 - 857 AD)**

   Imam Hanbal born in Marw (Iraq), was the youngest of the founders of the four schools of thought in Islamic law. He had the advantage of studying all the works of his predecessors. With the aid of all the highly developed facilities of his mind, he attempted a scientific and critical approach to the study of law. Like Imam Al-Shafi'i, he disagreed with the philosophical ideas of the mutazilites (free thinkers) of the Abbasid Caliphate. He was persecuted for his conscience under the rule of the Abbasids. He believed strongly that the Qu'ran is the knowledge of Allah and was therefore not created but inspired and therefore the law which derives from it must be divine.

When the news of his persecution and his refusal to surrender his belief in the Qu'ran reached Imam Bukhari in Basrah, he was reported have remarked with pride "If Imam Hanbal had been born a Jew, perhaps he would have been counted as one of the Prophets of Allah". Among his many works, the most prominent were: Kitab al-Amal, Kitab al-Tafsir, Kitab al- Nisikh al-Mensukh, Kitab al-Zahid, Kitab al-Masa'iI, Kitab al-Fada'il, Kitab al-Mansik and Kitab al-Imam. The best known of his major works is Al-Musnad which is a collection of some 700,000 ahadith.

The four orthodox Sunni schools of thought had profound influence in the development of Islamic jurisprudence, Islamic theology and Constitutional theory. In his Book, Shariah the Islamic Law, Abdur Rahman I Dci, observed that "by the end of the 9th century these schools of thought had come to subscribe to a common theory, namely that the main sources of Islamic law are the Qur'an and its interpretations by Prophet Mohammed and eminent Islamic scholars and jurists.

The famous Islamic theologians who founded the four schools of thought succeeded in dividing Sharia into five broad categories - namely:

(a) Akidat (belief)
(b) Adab (moralities)
(c) Ibadatu (devotions)
(d) Mu'amalat (transactions)
(e) Ukubat (punishments).

These five categories come under two broader divisions -namely (a) urn-al Kalam (dealing with all matters of faith), and (b) Ilm-al fiqh (this includes all matters of practice as distinct from matters of faith). It is this second division that Canon law comes close to but still remains distinct from it.

To suggest that the entrenchment of Sharia in the Nigerian Constitution is synonymous with the commencement of the islamization of the society is to ignore the lessons of history in the spread of [slam in Nigeria and elsewhere. Few would argue against the historically proven fact that a good part of Europe was, in the past, occupied by the Muslims for some five hundred to eight hundred years. However, even the most critical historical records of this period of Muslim occupation reveal no shred of evidence of any attempt, direct or otherwise, to islamize Europe. With the exception of two short colonial intercessions by France and Britain, Egypt has been governed by Muslims for the best part of 1,500 years. Yet, in a country whose total population is surrounded by Muslims and Islamic influence, exists a thriving community of over 10 million coptic Christians, rejected by the rest of Christendom, but tolerated by Islam.

Islam came to Northern Nigeria as early as the 7th century but up to the early part of the 20th century, when the British occupied Nigeria, there was no evidence whatsoever of any attempt by Muslims to force non-Muslims to accept either their religion or their way of life. Even though it may leave those of other faiths dumbfounded, there is, and has always been, no compulsion in Islam. In fact, no other major religion accords as much respect to the tenets and followers of other religions as does Islam. Muslims consider Christians and Jews to be their fellow worshippers in slightly different interpretations of the same monotheistic religious view. The socio-cultural distinctions, the practical differences and the variations in detail are all accepted and respected by Muslims.

Issues such as Nigeria's membership of the OIC or the activities of the Nigeria's Pilgrim's Board would under normal circumstances not come under the purview of this study, but because they attracted undue attention during the debate on the new constitution, there is need to examine them in the right perspective. A constitution, being a legal document, is concerned mainly with the legitimate functions of government and its agencies. Government actions which appear in conflict with the spirit of the constitution are construed as unconstitutional. It is in this light we must examine these two controversial issues in our attempt to understand the theoretical basis of government's action in the issues under consideration. This will facilitate our understanding of the Decalogue which defines our duty toward God and toward ourselves. Since the Decalogue constitutes a central theme in the making of a people, that is, both religious and political, then all governmental actions must be interpreted accordingly. Convenant in a political sense is what Rousseau refers to as "social contract". By implication human convenants are not "contracts' with precise requirements and guarantees, but more of unconditional pledges for loyalty, protection and service to the people. It would be instructive to begin treating the OIC issue by asking a simple rhetorical question.

If the establishment of diplomatic relations with and the appointment of an Ambassador to the Holy See (a purely theocratic Roman Catholic city state) does not christianize any country, one is forced to wonder why some individuals remain convinced that an act such as joining the Organization of Islamic Conference (OIC), which has many non-Muslims states as its members, would islamize Nigeria. One of the best tests of an organization is its aims and objectives. There is nothing in its objectives or the nature of its membership to indicate that it is set up to islamize its members. It cannot be denied that the organization began with some limited regional, political and economic objectives, but its increased membership has necessarily transformed it into a truly international organization. Its objectives were, therefore, modified and expanded accordingly. Article II of the Organization's Charter reads:

> the objectives of the organization are clearly stated to wit: To consolidate cooperation among member states in the economic, social, cultural, scientific and other vital fields of activities; to carry out consultations among member states in international organizations; to endeavour to eradicate colonialism in all its forms; to take necessary measures to support international peace and security founded on justice and to create a suitable atmosphere for the promotion of co-operation and understanding among member states and other countries.

We all know that any analysis confined to the "objective" situation misses the point that individuals and groups make decisions on the basis of their appraisal of a situation and that this may not correspond to some objective definition of reality.

It seems evident from the articles of association of the. organization that it is first and foremost an international economic, co-operation institution designed to be of benefit to all citizens of its member countries. It was not established to be of more benefit to Muslim citizens to the exclusion of their Christian brothers. This argument is also true of Nigeria's relationship with the Holy See, (Vatican) which is of benefit to both christians and their muslim brothers. This seems to explain why so many non-Muslim developing states such as Senegal, Guinea, Uganda, Benin, Sierra Leone, Burkina Faso, Chad, Gabon, Gambia, Comoros Island, some of whose muslim populations are meagre chose to join the OIC. Indeed a precursor to membership is having some Islamic populations, but the benefits to be gained are universal. It does not seem realistic to suggest that the member countries are likely to become Islamized because of their membership, nor is it fair to say that their leaders acted on inadequate information for their decision, or were incapable of comprehending fully what the membership of the organization entails? It would seem more reasonable to suggest that the need for economic cooperation and the genuine desire to raise the standards of living of their people must have led to the decision of each to join the international organization. Reason rather than emotion should have dictated our stand on the OIC issue. After all, if any advantages were to accrue as a result of membership of the organization, it is not the Muslims alone who would benefit from them but Nigerian society as a whole.

It is contended by some that Nigeria surreptitiously upgraded her position in OIC without making the decision public. Whatever the Government's position on this issue is, it is work understanding the process of decision-making in establishing diplomatic relations with foreign countries and joining international organizations. Any such endeavour is usually based on a well reasoned ministerial initiatives. Indeed such initiatives are usually followed by government s endorsement. They are not arbitrary decisions made by individuals based on religious bigotry, lack of concern for and insensitive to the manner in which the public is to apt to interpret the decision of government. The officials involved in the decision-making process must have been acutely aware of the possibility of misperception by the public.

The public is of course entitled to know the rationale behind government s decision to establish relations with any country or organization. It is interesting to note that the decision to establish relations with the Holy See was never contested by any member of the Nigerian public when the facts became known? It must have been because the public found it to have been based on sound judgement and that the end result was found to be in the spiritual interest of Nigerian Christians and therefore in the public interest. Similarly the hosting of these visits of the Pope and Archbishop of Cantarbury to Nigeria at the public's expense was never contested by any Muslim. The Muslim community must have concluded that the special spiritual function and significance of the visits to the Christian community of fellow Nigerians warranted both government effort and expenditure in the realization of the visits. It is significant to note that the Muslims have no established international religious figures comparable to the Pope and the Archbishop to be invited, due to the more decentralized method of operation of the Islamic system. Had this not been so, one would have hoped that the same objective reasoning should hold in respect of any effort aimed at strengthening Nigeria's external ties with such eminent individuals, regardless of the fact that the whole populace does not share their religious convictions.

The circumstances leading to the appointment of a Nigerian envoy to the Vatican deserves a special mention because it demonstrates how a government can go out if its way to satisfy the yearnings of a section of its society. This case is often ignored but it is crucial to a better understanding of how a government reacts to such situations. When it became impossible, for reasons of protocol, to concurrently accredit the Nigerian Ambassador to Italy to the Vatican, the Government had to find some other acceptable alternative country for the purpose of concurrent accreditation. Spain qualified both in terms of proximity to the Vatican and from the point of view of being a Catholic State. Relations are normally established between countries either because of considerable levels of consular activities created by the presence of the other country's nationals in each country's territory, appreciable economic activities between the two states or special strategic or political relations. As far as Spain was concerned, none of these factors was of any significance at the time diplomatic relations with Nigeria were established. The only overriding reason was to find a suitable place for an Ambassador who could be concurrently accredited to the Vatican. It is important to note the fact that since the establishment of relations with Spain, no non-Christian envoy has ever been appointed to that country.

Muslim officials participated in the excise leading to this understanding but none of them saw the case as one in which government acted covertly or overtly in favour of one religion. The unanimous view was that the action was in the overall interest of Nigeria.

The activities of the Nigerian Pilgrim's Board must be viewed with considerable degree of objectivity. The term pilgrim tends to evoke religious sentiment and this in turn tends to colour our judgment on the true meaning of the activities of the Board. The decision to add pilgrimage to Rome and Jerusalem to the activities of the Board was meant to remove any elements of discrimination by government in the treatment of its citizens.

This action merely mitigated, but did not eliminate the emotional element which gave rise to the initial criticism of government's involvement in the activities of the Board. Ideally, the Nigerian Pilgrim's Board ought to be seen for what it really is. It is for all intents and purposes a consular agency established to assist the government in protecting her nationals and their properties abroad. This function is the first duty of a country's diplomatic mission abroad. The function involves protecting the lives and promoting the interests and welfare of nationals residing or travelling abroad no matter what the purpose of their travel may be. The nationals are entitled to this service irrespective of their religion and for reason the board serves a legitimate function which no government can afford to abandon. To see this function in any other light is to ignore the realities of government responsibility to its citizens which they are abroad for whatever reason. An agreement reached at Geneva (Geneva Convention) places legal responsibility on all governments, who are party to the agreement to protect or evacuate their nationals if the need arises, offer legal aid whenever its citizens are in jail, protect their properties and interests if foreign governments cannot provide such services. Consulates are essentially diplomatic substations established to serve travellers to and from host countries.

It would enhance our understanding of consular responsibilities of modern governments if we examine the role foreign consular missions play during tourist season in Europe. The staff and funds of most European and American diplomatic missions in Spain, Portugal, Greece, Italy, Israel and Gibralter are beefed up to meet the needs of their nationals who flood those Mediterranean countries during the tourist season. The basic aim of a tourist is enjoyment, yet his government is obliged to come to his aid from the time he intends to travel until he gets back home. It would be recalled that before independence, Britain carried out consular duties in the Sudan, France and Spain on behalf of Nigeria. Late Ambassador John Garba, a devout Nigerian christian was proud to be the first Nigerian to take consular duty for Nigerian at the British Embassy in Khartum just before Nigerian independence. He saw his duty as purely service to his fellow country men passing through the Sudan to the Muslim Holy Land. He never saw his actions as aiding Islam (see his book - *The Time jIas Come*), but service to his country. This should be the view of all Nigerians toward pilgrims, be they Christians or Muslims.

Very little is known of the annual pilgrimage that takes place within Nigeria itself. At least some 50,000 (fifty thousand) Nigerians are known to visit the tomb of Othman Dan Fodio at Sokoto every year. Similarly, large numbers of Nigerians visit Shrines and other religious sites in other parts of the country annually. It is interesting to note that neither the Federal nor State governments gets involved in these visits. The visits are of local nature and for this reason no consular duty is involved. Such travels are therefore of no interest to any government and as such they occur unnoticed.

Much of the confusion surrounding the activities of the Nigerian Pilgrims Board emanated from lack of understanding of the extent of government responsibilities to its citizens. The responsibility of the Board begins not only when the pilgrims are abroad but right from home. The entire process involved in the preparation for the travel is a consular function. It starts with the issue of passports, examination for medical fitness, issue of international health certificates, relevant information on what obtains in the countries citizens intend to visit.

CHAPTER 4

THE SOURCES OF COMMON LAW

The views often expressed about the backgrounds of the legal systems that operate in Nigerian society reveal a considerable degree of misunderstanding amongst the participating commentators in their discussions. For example, the view is held among some Nigerians that Common Law is not Christian Law, but the product of pre-Christian England. In essence, it is seen as an amalgam of the diverse customary laws of England.

Reasonable men of all persuasions are bound to find it difficult to understand the basis of this view since English customary laws are known to be decayed and were replaced by Christian laws. If this had been the view of laymen, one could have said that is was excusable because of their ignorance of the background of Common Law. However, coming from supposedly well-informed sources, as it often does, this view raises a number of vital questions which must be answered if this fundamental misunderstanding between Nigerian Christians and Muslims is to be resolved. Amongst the questions which must be answered are - what is Common Law and what are its sources? History tells us that with the coming of Common Law to England, the judiciary discouraged the continuance of localism and local custom in law to the detriment of Common Law. Local customs had to be claimed and proved, and where they were in conflict with Common Law, they were adjudged invalid. In discussing comparative law, the *Encyclopaedia Britannica* confirmed this view when it concludes that "local laws were no more than rubbish and evidently bound to decay". Thus, to see pre- Christian English customary laws as valid today, is to indulge in mere parochialism and a vain belief in the sacredness of the everlasting inviolability of law. It must be said, in all honesty, that such precepts are no longer valid or of interest to scholars interested in giving society a model of ideal justice or elucidating a higher law above man's making. It is important to know that none other than the most authoritative Christian theologians and unimpeachable, objective documentary sources describe *Common Law as "Christian Law"*.

Research has shown clearly that the most significant influence on the Western philosophy of law and jurisprudence were Saint Augustine, Emperor Justinian I and Saint Thomas Aquinas. Their highly authoritative works clearly highlight the direct connection between the Christian religion and Common Law.

It is generally recognized that among the most important considerations in the philosophy of Western law is that of the distinction between law and its moral dimension (*New Encyclopaedia Britannica* (vol 5, (1984) pp. 712-715) The questions that were known to have preoccupied the minds of the early great theological/legal philosophers were:

(a) How far should the law of a community seek to give effect to its morality?
(b) Is there a moral duty to obey the law even when it is inconsistent with morality?
(c) Is there a duty to overthrow an entire legal system because it is in conflict with morality.

The key issue in all these questions is "morality". Morality here denotes the community's relevant factual behaviour pattern (its mores), its socially approved behaviour as sanctified by religious ideals and the moral ideals which individuals accept as binding upon themselves. We all know that subsequent developments in natural law from the Renaissance to the 20th Century were greatly influenced by the growth of the social sciences, but throughout this period Catholics have maintained a strict stand on legal institutionalism.

They regard social institutions such as the family or the cooperative organization as expressions of social reality underlying the law. It is generally agreed that for the Catholics, the fundamental assumptions of natural law are evident in the insistence on "the principles of organization", the "communion" of members in realizing "durable ideals". They see these principles as essential elements of any institution, legal or social. (Ibid, pp. 710- 720). It is for this reason that legal philosophers such as Maurice Hauriou, Georges Renard and Leon Duguit (all French Catholics) see the principles of justice as the principles of social organization inherent and self-evident in natural law. It would be recalled that even though the protestants have rejected some of the books of the Old Testament, this rejection does not extend to the biblical source of the established principles on which the concept of justice if based. In other words, there was an almost total unanimity amongst all Christian denominations on the established legal principles. It is worth shedding some light on how and when these principles were established.

(a) St. Augustine of Hippo (354 - 430 AD)

St. Augustine of Hippo is generally recognized as the greatest thinker of Christian antiquity. In an attempt to refute the pagan allegation that the church was responsible for the fall of the Roman Empire, St. Augustine set out to fuse stoic philosophy with Christian theology. In his description of the Kingdom of God (see - *City of God*), he developed an elaborate system of laws and offices adapted to the temporal world. He developed the concepts of natural and divine law. His success in introducing stoic philosophy alongside Judeo-Christian thought into the mainstream of modern jurisprudential speculation has left a permanent mark on the Western concept of law. His theory of law has remained the most authoritative source of Common Law in Christian Europe and wherever in the world their influence spread. Nigeria, as coincidence will have it just happens to be one of those areas that came to be influenced by the concept of Common Law.

St. Augustine, for his part, has left no one in any doubt as to the origin of his monumental works on law. His main source was the Holy Bible, more specifically, the first five books of the Old Testament: namely, Genesis, Exodus, Leviticus, Numbers and Deuteronomy. According to eminent Christian scholars, these books are the "Books of Law" in the Bible (see one of St. Augustine's major works - *The Confessions*). Augustine attempted a systematic Christian philosophy of society. In his *City of God* he developed an ideal legal system in which the state mediates between the earthly realm of sin and disharmony and the heavenly realm of absolute righteousness. St Augustine argued that in a world infested by the imperfections of avarice and greed, the state must subject society to the discipline of justice. In his view, an ideal state which is capable of instilling this discipline is where there exist the rule of free men by free men. The rule is through deliberation guided by nature and by God. Any situation to the contrary would, in the view of St. Augustine, lead to a violation of natural order and divine law! The situation of absolute righteousness depicted in the *City of God* is a reincarnation of Plato's *Republic* and is also the ancestor of Christian doctrines of natural justice. St Augustine was a pioneer in the field of international law. He attempted to develop principles of international dispute by presenting a thought-provoking analysis of peace at three levels - (a) the peace of God, (b) the peace of the just, and (c) the peace of the unjust (war). St Augustine's work had a profound and lasting influence on Christian thought and practice. Today, Augustianism is the name given to the tradition of Christian politics inspired by the City of God and for the coherent doctrine and policy governing relations between Church and State.

(b) Emperor Justinian I. (483 - 565 AD)

Roman Emperor Justinian I was one of the greatest jurists Europe ever had. Unlike St. Augustine, he was not a theologian, but an academician, one of unquestionable repute, without doubt. His greatest achievements in the field of law were his collection and codification of the laws, edicts, decrees and other orders issued by Roman authorities over hundreds of years. According to the *New Encyclopaedia Britannica* vol.4 (pp. 998 - 1005), from a theological point of view, the most significant aspect of his immense contribution to the development of Common Law (then known as Roman Law) was his stringent ecclesiastical policy which supported orthodoxy and led him to centre his deliberations on the parameters of the concepts of law developed by St. Augustine. Justinian's fame was said to have rivaled that of Aristotle and Maimonides. St. Aquinas likened him to a "Rabbi" (Priest) (see Justinian's works - *The Digests and Institutes* - both published in 533 AD).

(c) St. Thomas Aquinas (1226 - 1274)

Aquinas was a prominent member of the St. Augustine Order in the Church. He was one of the greatest of the medieval theologians and was a philosopher of law and politics. It was he who developed the modern concept of *Common Law.* Like St. Augustine, he strove to accommodate both natural and temporal law in eternal law. Aquinas did not concern himself with particular laws or edicts, but with the principles of all laws. He was not content with only human law, but brought all kinds of law under his purview - human, divine, eternal and natural law (see his greatest work on law - *Summa Theological*). Both St. Aquinas and St. Augustine relied on the five "Sacred Books" of the Bible referred to above, otherwise known as the Pentateuch, for his definition, development and refinement of the concept of law.

He generated an authoritative system of theological, moral and political ideology which served as the foundation for Roman Catholic teaching. His political philosophy consists of an elaborate elucidation of the doctrine of natural justice.

Aquinas based his theory of law on the premise that Divine Law consists of God's commandments as revealed in the scriptures. Unlike other thinkers of his time , Aquinas believed that natural law is sufficient in itself to generate all positive law. Positive law (human law) consists of the particular legal enactments that rational beings make for the good government of their institutions. Aquinas believed also that natural law generates a human law of private property which if violated leads to injustice.

Aquinas insisted that the effect of law is to lead people to their true virtue and through law a perfect community can be attained. He distinguished himself by his efforts in expanding the concept of natural law and extending it into the sphere of commerce and international relations. In commerce, he developed the theory of just price in international trade. In international relations, he continued the work of St Augustine by laying down rules of just dealing between states and he defined the nature of just war. The distinction he made between different types of war and just dealings between enemies underlie the intellectual structure of the modern law of war.

The works of these great intellectual giants, with their basis firmly entrenched in their respective interpretation of the Sacred Books of the Bible, are the best known sources of Common Law as we know it today.

It is believed that the term "Common Law" itself was first used by the Greek philosopher Plato when he compared man to a puppet whose movements are controlled by strings and cords. According to him, among the cords, there is the golden cord of reason which he called *Common Law of State*. It was left to St. Aquinas to refine the concept for application in the modern European legal system.

It is only against this background that the statement by a British member of the House of Lord Summer, in *Bowman Vs Secular Society Ltd* (1917 Appeal Cases 406) which suggested that English law may well be called Christian law, can be fully understood. By implication, Lord Summer confirmed the fact that the source of Common Law (English Law), was Christian theology. After all he had no reason to deny it. The only logical conclusion that is possible to draw from this is that English Common Law is inherently Christian in all its facets. This same conclusion was reached by Hugh Trevor-Roper in his book titled *Renaissance Essays* (page 32). Even the mode of dress of English Lawyers and Judges must have had its origin from the Church of England. Nigeria has inherited this entire tradition through colonial education.

G. D. Nokes attests to the fact that Common Law is Christian Law when he states in his book *An Introduction to Evidence*:

> Coke repeated some of the older learnings about oaths, holding that non-Christians, whom he called infidels, were unable to be witness because Christians oaths would not bind them. But the number of such persons in late medieval England was small, and their appearance in the ordinary courts unusual: so the theory probably had little practical value... This was not difficult in the case of Jews because they professed belief in the same God, if not the same triune Godhead, as Christians and some of their sacred books formed part of the Bible. It was decided that they could be sworn as witnesses on the Old Testament (p. 300-39 1).

The statement credited to Dr Jonah Madugu (*Sunday Standard* of 20th November, 1988) to the effect that Muslim judges have accepted positions in the Common Law system in Nigeria only because the law is not Christian is misleading. The view expressed is not supported by any empirical evidence and appears to be derived primarily from the commentator's limited knowledge regarding the nature of Islamic beliefs. The Qur'an teaches all Muslims to believe in Moses and Jesus Christ and their teachings and their books, Torah and Injil respectively. No Muslim is a real Muslim unless he does so. This simply means the position of the handful of Muslim judges in Common Law courts which are Christian Courts, is not inconsistent with their basic religious beliefs. On the contrary, it is Christian judges who would find their position in Islamic Courts totally at variance with their basic religious beliefs in that they neither believe in Prophet Muhammad nor in the Qur'an.

Only recently (23rd December 1988) Sir Patrick Maykey, the British Attorney-General, reconfirms that Common Law is Christian Law when he informed the Muslims in Britain who wanted Salman Rushdie, the author of *The Satanic Verses* and his publishers to be prosecuted for blasphemy that the book constitutes no criminal offence in England because "blasphemy law of England only caters for Christianity and the law could not be changed". (*Newswatch* 6th March, 1989, p. 29).

CHAPTER 5

COMMON LAW IN NIGERIA

The Common law which operates in Nigeria was directly imported from England, but, more important than where it came from, or the manner in which it evolved are the established *principles* upon which it has developed. The supremacy of Common Law in England was neither easily or quickly achieved.

Cardinal Thomas Wolsey who fell from the favour of the king was in 1529 accused of attempting to import Roman Law into England. Lord Coke, the famous English jurist emphasized in Bonham's case, in 1610, the tradition that was based on the assumption that "when an act of Parliament is against common right or reason or repugnant or impossible to be performed, the Common Law will control it, and adjudge such an act to be void". History further tells us that, a century before Lord Coke's statement, an English treatise, known as *St. Germain, Doctor and Student*, had already developed a three-tier hierarchy of the law of God, natural and human law.

Authoritative sources have confirmed that these laws are quite clearly derived from St. Augustine and St. Aquinas. History also tells us that, under the Roman Empire, the law was called *Christian Roman Empire Law*. It was after the fall of the Roman Empire that the words "*Christian*" *and* "*Roman Empire*" were discarded. According to the E*ncyclopaedia Britannica*, Vol. 10 (pp. 714-722) there were two simple reasons for these developments.

Firstly, the Roman Empire no longer existed. Therefore, association with it was no longer necessary nor was it desirable. Secondly, there were virtually no more pagans left in Europe by this time. Paganism in Europe was finally destroyed between 378 and 420 AD. This, therefore removed the need to distinguish the Christian from pagan laws.

An understanding of the history of Nigerian Common Law must assume a basic knowledge of British society in which it functioned in an earlier age from here. English Law (later known as Common Law) was greatly influenced by the laws of Justinian I (Roman Law). As the rich and varied Anglo Saxon Law began to break-down in England, the scope of Roman Law increased considerably. Admiralty Law, for example, drew on Greek, Roman and Italian Law. Certain types of crime such as forgery and libel were all dealt with according to Roman models. Wales and Northern England were governed by Roman Law. Lord Mansfield, recognize4 as one of the most charismatic and able law-makers to sit in an English Court, had profound influence on Common Law. He broadened it by infusing into it elements of other legal systems. By the late 19th Century, when the extraordinary influence of Sir Williams Blackstone in the development and dissemination of Common Law to other parts of the world became well recognized, the scope of the influence of Roman Law ideas in England had assumed greater proportions than was generally realized. In other words, the concept of Common Law had become truly and thoroughly christianized well before it was imported to Africa (including Nigeria) in early 20th Century.

Our discussions have so far revealed that the principles upon which English Law and, by association, Nigerian Common Law developed are not simply Christian inspired, but in fact, Judeo-Christian in origin and content (the Books of the Holy Bible). These principles have remained unchanged since the time they were being developed by the likes of St. Augustine of Hippo, St Thomas Aquinas and Justinian I. It is not, therefore, at all reasonable to deny that Common Law is "Christian Law" or to say what operates in Nigeria today is a pre-Christian English law. The following paragraphs will give us some idea of the fate of English Customary Law in the wake of the advent of Common Law and the role of the Church in its development in England.

The theory that the king is the "fountain of justice" began with the Norman Conquest (1066). Anglo-Saxon justice was local in that trials were held locally in county courts by the king's representatives sent out from Curia Regis, and the tenants-in-chief. The presiding officer at the courts sessions was usually a leading cleric. George W. Keeton records in his book, *English Law*, that names that most frequently appeared in the court transcripts are Lanfranc, Arch Bishop of Canterbury, the Bishop of Bayeux and the Bishop of Countenances. The justices were sent out from the king's Central Court and were either lay or clerical rather than professional lawyers.

It was during the reign of the resourceful English king, Henry II, that the development of Common Law began. Henry II was an Angevin and not a Norman. He ruled lands on both sides of the English Channel (England and Normandy) each with its own distinctive culture, administration and systems of law. Increases in business and the diversity of the legal systems led to the establish of two Common Law courts (King's Bench and the Common Pleas). With this new development judicial work became distinct from other kinds of administrative work and it came to be administered in conformity with settled principles (those established by St Augustine and St Aquinas). It is important to note that the justices were still royal administrators (barons) and clerics in *holy orders* who received the normal reward of ecclesiastical preferments.

The history of English Law confirms that, at the time of Magna Carta, clerics overwhelmingly predominated the king's courts. In fact the literature of English Law was known to have been written by men who were clerics. Bracton is the best example of a cleric who played significant roles in the king's courts and received the reward of ecclesiastical preferments. He was Justice of Assize, Justice in eye and Justice of the King's Bench. He studied Civil and Common Law in Italy under the tutelage of the Italian jurist, Azo. Bracton's work is reported to be firmly based upon Common law and has influenced the judges of succeeding centuries.

The reign of Henry III marked the beginning of a professional and cooperate approach to English Law. The proportion of clerics to lay judges decreased. Throughout his reign nineteen judges served in the courts and only eight of them were lay judges. The reign of Edward II was transitional as far as the development of Common Law is concerned, but even then the clerics were prominent in the judiciary. A very distinguished Chief Justice of the Common Pleas, Ralph of Hengham was a cleric. Chief Justice Harvey de Stanton who succeeded the famous Chief Justice Sir William Bereford in 1326, was another cleric.

The real turning point in the development of the English medieval judiciary began with the reign of Edward III. His reign saw a major change in English legal development. Even though appointments of clerics as judges went well into this period, but never again would clerics of Harvey de Stanton's stature occupy important positions in the judiciary. The secularization of the King's Bench made it possible for more professional lawyers to practice in the King's courts. The fifth Lateran Council forbade the clergy to practice in the secular courts, except in their own causes or on behalf of the poor. Once the clerics on the bench and in practice of law had gone, the profession began to develop a vigorous character of its own, much of which has survived to this day.

The importance of our discussion so far is that, throughout the transition of English Medieval judiciary to Common Law, clerics had dominated the sphere of the administration of justice in England. Even when Common Law was gaining ground throughout England, there was evidence of a clear link between the Exchequer and clerical justices receiving ecclesiastical preferments. As has been stated, during the reign of Edward II, the bench was still shared between clerics and lay lawyers. This means clerical judges, often eminent and learned, made immense contributions to the earliest phase of the development of the Common Law. What is of particular interest to us is that the evidence shows that the ecclesiastical principles of law developed by the early Christian theologians have almost totally survived all the changes in the development of English Common Law which Nigeria has inherited. It is the selfsame set of principles that governs the Common Law system which operates in the Nigerian society today.

The secularization of the judiciary in England did not mean that the legal system was purged of its Christian content. English legal scholarship was enriched by the organic growth of continental canonists. It is quite clear that learning in Canon Law went hand in hand with learning in Roman Law. Famous English prelates such as Warham, Morton and Wolsey were of the highest repute as Canonists. An important thing to remember is that for the English judges in the early days, there was no discernible difference between their outlook upon Common Law and that of Canon Law. We need to bear in mind that the letters LLB, which represent a law degree, stand for the Latin for "Bachelor of Both Laws", i.e Canon and Civil law. History also tells us that although the teaching of Canon Law was prohibited at Reformation, universities continued to turn their back on English Law until the second half of the 18th Century. Even though, in the jurisdiction of English Courts, Christianity was confined to spiritual matters, their influence on civil and criminal law has survived to this day. The influence of Canon Law upon the developed fabric of English Law has been far more extended than is generally conceded. For example, the influence of the Church in establishing the principles of marriage, nullity and separation can hardly be overrated. It would be recalled that the rule relating to nullity and separation were maintained as the basis of English Law of Marriages several centuries after the Reformation. Keeton reminds us that even after Parliament had, in 1857, established a special divorce court with jurisdiction to grant divorces, the grounds for a petition still owed much to Canon Law principles. This also applies to the principle that marriage was the monogamous union of life- long duration.

Another fact that is often forgotten is that the secularization of the judiciary in nearly the whole of Europe was, to some extent, a product of clash of interest between the church and European rulers. Each was prepared, in principle, to advance the interest of the other, but where these interests clashed the rulers tended to have their way. In England, for example, struggles between Henry II and his rebellious Archbishop, Thomas A Backet, led to the "Constitutions of Clarendon" which regulated the spheres of the Crown and Church. Similarly, the clash between Henry VIII and his Chancellor, Sir Thomas More, led to the break with Rome and the evolution of the Anglican Church with the English monarch as its new head. It will be recalled that the Church ruled Europe for centuries. The Pope, in his capacity as the political and spiritual head of Europe (Holy Roman Emperor), appointed and deposed European Emperors and kings. The Papal influence over Europe helped to christianize their legal system well before the Reformation. It is inconceivable that the clerics who dominated the legal system for centuries would administer any laws, other than Christian laws. It was only a matter of time before that the remnants of pagan and customary laws were swept away by the tide of Common Law.

It would seem logical to conclude that no amount of subsequent reforms can eradicate the indelible influence of the Christian theological principles upon which the European legal systems developed right from the 4th Century. The difficulties encountered in the development of Common Law were the changes in the structures and procedure of the European machinery of justice. The principles upon which justice rests have not changed since the days of the eminent theologians - St Augustine and St Aquinas - and this is what makes Common Law Christian Law. To deny that it is, is to turn one's blind eye to reality and reason. It is misleading to assume that the legal reforms of the 1830s had changed the basic principles of law which were established in the 4th and 5th Century. Alexander Llevethyn in his book, *the Decade of Reform*, reminds us that the reforms were necessary in order to reflect the changes taking place in England - a new social order characterized by the acceptance of the concept of democracy, principles of liberty, emergence of a two-party system, moves towards a local government system, industrial expansion, heavy investment overseas, colonization, political and industrial agitation. Social problems created by all these new and unforeseen developments had to be accommodated in the English legal system. This necessitated not only a substantial restructuring of the structures and procedures of the legal system, but also the elucidation and refinement of the basic legal concepts upon which justice was administered. The structural changes emanating from these social changes did not lead to any noticeable changes in the principles of English laws as enunciated by the early Christian theologians.

What is not often realized is that it is quite easy to confuse Common Law with its rules of pleading and practice. This seems to be the source of confusion in the Nigeria's view of law. Common Law must be seen as a complete developed and self-sufficient system of law which possesses its own basic principles and doctrines. It is these principles and doctrines which make the heart of the law. Common Law must therefore not be seen as merely a collection of rules and practice which can be compendiously pieced together in tracts. Rules and established practice are, of course, very important in that they make the law practical and capable of adaptation to meet the needs of a dynamic and rapidly changing society. It is for this reason that the rules become readily more complex because they cover a wide range of specialized legal logic. This is necessarily so because the rules are founded upon the actual problems of daily life in a society.

Littleton's *Tenures*, the first famous book on Common Law not written in Latin, was highly commended by Sir Edward Coke as easily the best and absolute work on human science. Following this work, professional lawyers played a key role in refining the rules of Common Law. The *New Tenures*, written in Norman- French is believed by many to be the best work on law. Common Law had, in the hands of professional lawyers, turned in upon itself in the middle of the 15th Century England.

To understand the source of our difficulties in interpreting divine law correctly, we must examine carefully the views of early theologians on law. In answering a thought provoking question posed by the Pharisees about the relationship between human positive law and divine law, Jesus replied:

> "...Render therefore unto Caesar the thing which are Caesar's and unto God the things that ai~ God's" (Matthew 22:2 1)

This answer appears deceptively simple and this must have led to the different interpretations of what Jesus actually meant.

Some have argued that the admission that certain things belong to Caesar is an indication that secular authority has a definite place in human life. Others argue that by reminding us that certain things are God's Jesus condemned the completely secular state. Those who support the latter view argue that the circumstances under which Jesus answered the Pharisees called for a careful consideration of the answer to the question. Two important facts need to be borne in mind. First, the human law in question was Roman law because Judea was then under temporal Roman authority. Second, the Pharisees life had all along been dictated by divine law (Laws of Moses). The question arises as to which law, Roman or divine, should dictate the life of the Pharisees. Would obedience to one of the laws imply disobedience to the other? It is important to remember that Roman laws then were pagan laws.

In his analysis on the question of relationship between the law in the Old Testament and New Testament, St Aquinas argues:

> ".. two laws may be distinguished from another in two ways.
>
> First, through being altogether different from the fact that they are ordered to different ends... Second, two laws may be distinguished from one another through one of them being more closely connected with the end and the other more remotely" (Summa Theological, Vol. 20, p. 326b)

Then he went further to elaborate:

> "...according to the first way the New law is not distinct from the Old Law because they both have the same end, namely, man's subjection to God .... According to the second way, the New Law is distinct from the Old Law, because the Old Law is like a pedagogue of children ... while the New Law is the law of perfection, since it is the law of charity" (Ibid, p. 326c)

St Paul appears much more direct and simpler in his answer to the question of relationship between the two laws:

> "the law is holy, and the commandment holy, and just, and good" (Romans 7:12)

St Aquinas definition of law offers some relief in the face of seemingly conflicting view of the Old-New and human laws. He writes:

> "Thus... the definition of law may be gathered; and it is nothing other than an ordinance of reason for the common good, made by him who has care of the community and promulgated" (Summa Theological Vol. 20, p. 208a)

On the distinction between human and divine law, St Aquinas asserts that men made human law and God made divine law and the two must therefore conform. St Aquinas admits that both Church and State have a function in man's life. This view puts a great deal of human conduct under the rule of divine law. If Christian religion regards all of man's life as a way toward God and some of his actions must be regulated by human law, then that law must be in accordance with divine law and should not contradict it. St Aquinas stresses the need for divine, positive law in the conduct of human affairs. He insists that the need for divine law arises from man's superior status in the hierarchy of creation and the fallibility and weakness of his powers.

It has been suggested that by his answer to the Pharisees, Jesus disavows the monolithic theocratic state and condemns the completely secular state. If this were so, then we must find an appropriate and acceptable meaning to the term secular state whenever we contemplate the adoption of one. We experience the greatest difficulties where divine and human law claim authority to regulate one and the same human action and when the precepts of these laws differ.

In elucidating the nature of the link between the kinds of precept of divine law and those of human law, St Aquinas argues that God intends to make men good by his law. Since the goodness of man is virtue, it follows that it was necessary for the laws in the Old Testament to include precepts about acts of virtue, and these are what became the moral precepts of law. St Aquinas went further to suggest that the moral precepts of the divine law command the same actions as the precepts of natural law. If natural law is unchangeable in its first principles, then the moral precepts of the law also do not change. This view is confirmed by Jesus Christ:

> "... out of the heart proceed evil thoughts, murders, adulteries, fornications, thefts, false witness, blasphemies: These are the things

which defile a man' (Matthew 15:19-20)

The need for these moral precepts, according to St Aquinas, arises from the defects of human reason. Human beings do not always or easily recognize what natural law expects of them, but the commandments of divine law are explicit and clear.

The question may well be asked: if the commandments of the divine law are really explicit and clear, why do we need the authority of the divine law to rescue man from his defects? St Aquinas answers this question when he observes:

> "human reason could not go astray in the universal principle, that is, as to the most common principles of the natural law, but through being habituated to sin, it became obscured in the point of things to be done in detail. But with regard to the other moral precepts, which are like conclusions drawn from the common principles of natural law, the reason of many men went astray, to the extent of judging to be lawful things that are in themselves."

This brings us back to the difficult point man must face about the event to which he can interpret or change the law without the risk of deviation from the basic common principles of natural or divine law. Our discussion leads us to the inevitable conclusion that human positive law cannot operate independently of its sources -divine and natural laws. In other words human law does not exist in a vacuum. Both statutes and common law undergo changes continuously, but the extent to which these changes can go has remained an unresolved problem of law. Since men live under natural law and the special function of human law consists of its pedagogical influence on society, it follows that law is an integral part of divine or natural law. St Aquinas confirms this when he says:

> "...since ... (they) are found to be depraved and prone to vice, and not easily amenable to words, it was necessary for such to be restrained from evil by force and fear, in order that at least they might cease from evil-

> doing and leave others in peace ... Now this kind of training, which compels through fear of punishment, is the discipline of laws"

The question which keeps recurring in our minds is where the line between divine law and human positive law is drawn. Experience has shown that every human action that has consequences for his moral perfection is ultimately a matter for the divine law. This necessarily means very little is left for human law to regulate man's actions. This then makes it difficult to determine the role a purely secular state is to play in regulating human affairs - as distinct from that which is to be played by religion - which is the source of all laws. The conclusion one can safely draw from this brief analysis is that human law cannot be separated from divine law and both must work together to aid man to attain virtue.

CHAPTER 6

The Relation Between Muslims And Non-Muslims In Islamic Law

An honourable member of the Constituent Assembly, a lawyer by profession, who was good enough to read the first manuscript of this work, drew attention to what he identified as an apparent omission in the list of issues against Sharia. He pointed out that one objectionable issue which was widely canvassed amongst Assembly members by some non-Muslim area members of some parts of the North is the occasional "compulsory' submission of some of their people to the jurisdiction of area courts". The writer did not consider this as an issue in the first place because of the impracticability, to his perception, of the allegation. The most likely explanation of the source of such misperception is from non-Muslims who would either like to believe or who have managed to convince themselves that this is how Muslims would treat non-Muslims. The truth is that it is obvious that such people know little about the administration of law in the North, and perhaps almost nothing about Islam and even less about Sharia itself. Clearly, one would want to know why such commentators feel qualified to comment on a delicate subject they have next to no knowledge about and no empirical evidence on. However, the fact that an eminent professional lawyer has been convinced by such claims to the extent that he feels that the issue should be discussed, makes the writer feel obliged to deal with the issue squarely. It will almost certainly be worth the effort, if the fear amongst non-Muslim in the country is a genuine one.

Any one familiar with the provisions of the Native Courts Law of 1956 and 1968 Area Court Edict would know that it is difficult, if not impossible, for a non-Muslim to be tried in Sharia Court against his wishes. It would be recalled that it was stated elsewhere in this work that there is no compulsion in Islam. This idea of non-compulsion applies also to the administration of Sharia. It therefore follows that no Sharia Court judge worth his position can compel a non-Muslim to his jurisdiction. This position is fundamental and absolutely intractable. It is well established that in the event of a case arising between a Muslim and a non-Muslim, the manner in which the case is ultimately conducted is dependent upon the nature of the case itself. A Sharia Court judge has three options open to him. He can refer the case to either a Common law Court or a Customary Court, if he is satisfied that the subject matter is not within Sharia jurisdiction. For example in a case involving land, the law applicable in the place where the land is located applies - situs - rather than the religion of the litigants.

The 1968 Area Court Edict created two types of Area Courts. One type is headed by a judge while the other by a President. The Edict provides for an Area Court, Upper Area Court and the Sharia Court of Appeal. The existence of a range of clear options open to litigants and the possibility of appeals distinguishes the Nigerian legal system from what obtains in the Sudan. An area of confusion which may well be responsible for the current misunderstanding in this area is where in a Sharia Court a Qadi ceases to be a judicial officer during a trial and becomes an arbiter instead. This situation can arise when a Qadi determines that he has no jurisdiction over a case and decides to invite experts in the local law which applies to a non- Muslim brought before him to participate in the trial. In such cases, the Qadi does not play the role of a judge but rather that of an arbiter. This system existed even before the advent of Common Law in Nigeria. This is the manner in which conflict of laws are resolved even in customary law courts in the Southern part of Nigeria. One would hope that it is therefore clear that no non-Muslim, according to the dictates of Sharia, can ever be tried in a Sharia Court against his will. There is always the right to appeal against such judgements if they occured.

A Sharia judge is always reminded by the advice of Sayyadina Umar Ibn Abdul-Aziz, who in his book, *Tabsiratu-el-Hukkam*, urges Muslim judges to administer justice in the light of what prevails in a given society.

When the question of imposition of law in Nigeria is raised, it is difficult to ignore the case of the Yoruba Muslims of former Western Nigeria under British administration. The impression is given that the Yoruba Muslim has voluntarily accepted Common Law jurisdiction instead of that of Islamic Law. A careful examination of the facts of what transpired in the Eastern and Western Provinces and the Colony of Lagos would reveal just the opposite. The British definition of Islamic Law, as is applied in Nigeria, is that it is part of native law and custom. This may be justified in the sense that Islamic Law has been practised in the Northern part of the country as far back as the 7th Century. What is often ignored is that it is not customary but a written law. Hence it has become a way of life for many Nigerian and as a consequence Islamic Law had been applied on territorial basis in the Muslim Emirates of the North. However, neither Islamic Courts nor any formal application of Islamic Law has been experienced in the South even in Yoruba land where the proportion of Muslims in the population is known to be high.

It is contended that, in general, there is little or no demand for the establishment of Muslim Courts or the application of Islamic Law in the South. It is further contended that the Yoruba Muslim appears contented to follow the religion of Islam in matters of doctrine and ritual but prefers to adhere to his tribal customs in such issues as marriage, divorce, adultery, guardianship and inheritance - deferring to Islamic Law only in cases of contracting marriages. These contentions are wrong in that they are not supported by the persistent efforts by the Yoruba Muslim communities to have Sharia Courts established in the Yoruba land (Anderson - Islamic Law in Africa, pp. 222-223). There was sufficient evidence to prove that as a result of the imposition of English Law, the Muslim Yorubas became more conscious of their religion and its law and expressed great concern about the consequences of any further disregard for its precepts.

Anderson records in his book the petition sent to the Chief Secretary to the Government of Nigeria by the Muslim Congress of Nigeria from its Secretariat in Ijebu-Ode:

> Muslims in the Southern Provinces of Nigeria have been deprived of the use of the ... just and moral code prescribed for use by the Holy prophet Muhammad .. for our guidance from generation to generation. It was high time this was changed because "our religion has been corrupted and many of our Muslim brothers have greatly gone astray while al-Qur'an, the Holy Book of Islam, has been badly and wrongly used by men who have no knowledge of it.

The Yoruba Muslims demanded in their petition for the establishment of a "Muslim Judiciary (Sharia) for southern Nigeria". This petition was followed by a stronger one addressed to the Brooke Commission in which the Yorubas indicated their desire to have the Sharia system developed in stages. First, it was to cover matrimonial and inheritance questions and subsequently marriage, divorce and other relevant matters currently dealt with by Native Courts. In this second petition the Yoruba Muslims requested fervently that their plea be accepted:

> We therefore pray this Commission to grant our request for a separate Muslim Court ... The condition of our courts is even worse in the case of law of inheritance. Our Native Authority civil court that grants letters of administration does not know any Muslim law governing this matter In conclusion, we have to say here that in almost all the towns and villages in the Western Provinces, Muslims are in the majority. For this fact, we request you kindly to consider our case sympathetically and to grant our request (Ibid p. 223).

The suggestion that the strength of the Yoruba tribal customs was the main obstacle to having the Sharia system established in the Yoruba land is also erroneous. Anderson admits that there was little support for the Yoruba Muslim demand because granting it would have, ostensibly caused confusion, but in reality, because it would also "raise a formidable obstacle to the ultimate fusion of native and English Law" (Ibid p. 223). This is where our problem lies. The more a society's norms and values are fused with alien ones the more that society loses its identity and the more vulnerable it becomes to outside manipulations during the course of its development.

In the Eastern Provinces where the Muslims were very few, there was no serious demand for the application of the Islamic Law. The Muslims were content to have a representative sit as an assessor in the native courts to protect the interests of fellow Muslim litigants. It seems logical to conclude that the deliberate attempt by the British colonial administrators to impose English Law on Nigerian society, more than any other factor, was responsible for the non-existence of Sharia Courts in Yoruba land, and, to a lesser extent, in the Eastern Provinces. Thus, the current controversy over Sharia is simply a reincarnation of British efforts and prejudice against the application of Islamic Law. If some Nigerians have accepted English Law because it is Christian Law and others have accepted Sharia because it is Islamic, then the problem is essentially one of coexistence of the two systems in the same environment. Certainly, the question is not simply that one is right and the other wrong.

The most practical solution lies in finding a way to accommodate the two sub-systems within an overall legal system acceptable to all Nigerians.

CHAPTER 7

CONFLICTING PERCEPTIONS OF A SECULAR STATE

We must now turn our attention to what the concepts of secularism and secularity actually entail and why, in Nigeria and elsewhere, there are conflicting views on them. *The Dictionary of Political Thought*, defines secularism as "a philosophy or doctrine that advocates the rejection of religion or the attitude that religion should have no place in civil affairs". On the other hand, the dictionary describes secularity as "a state of being not concerned with or related to religion or having no particular religious affinity". Indeed, there must be a host of other definitions of these concepts but they are all likely to centre around the same themes. The difference between the two concepts appears to be a matter of degree rather than substance. In any case, what is most important is what a state does in approach to religion and not what it simply calls itself. Let us examine what the secularity of a state entails.

Many Nigerians have failed to either understand or appreciate the position of the Muslims on the issue of secularity of the state whenever the concept is discussed. It is not generally known that, as a matter of principle, Muslims do not conceive of a view of life which is based on the premise that religion and religious considerations should be rejected, ignored or purposely excluded in their daily affairs in the name of progress. It is this view of secularity that Muslims find most disagreeable to their view of life. It is in sharp conflict with the Islamic legal system (Sharia) which they accept is a practical system based on divine guidance. The secularist, in this sense, envisages a process in which religious offices, institutions and ceremonies are removed from public life. The question being asked is that, in such a situation, what is the moral basis of these offices and institutions if their religious content is removed? A society must have some moral basis and any government that wishes to govern a society properly must take the moral basis into cognisance in its governance. It is for this reason that it is not enough to see a secular state merely as one in which government actions are not covertly or overtly religious. In considering what a secular state is or is not it is necessary to take into account the wider I implications of secularism from which it must have derived its nature and meaning. One essential difference in the conception of the Muslims and the Christians in Nigeria on this issue is clearly fundamental and must therefore be treated dispassionately.

Those who insist on the inviolability of Nigeria's secular status tend to see secularization of a state purely through the narrow definition of the concept in terms of the transfer of authority from religious institutions to secular bodies. As a concept, secularization has both its positive and negative aspects. It was a 16th Century European liberal concept which had its roots in the Reformation, during which Martin Luther (1483 - 1546) fought relentlessly not only for doctrinal reforms of the activities of the Church but also equality for his Lutheran Church in an atmosphere dominated wholly by the Catholic Church. In this sense, equality defines the relationship between the State and all Christian denominations. It began as a radical movement away from the traditional belief that man must think of God and life after death all the time. Adherents of the new concept, who were motivated by the idea of progress, began to believe that man ought to devote some time to attend to his worldly affairs. This idea was initially repugnant to the thinking of most Christians who interpreted the move as the beginning of a gradual disappearance of religious thought and feeling in man. For them to accept this change in the concept of religion was to confine it to an abstract worship of the transcendental.

Acceptance of the idea of secularity then meant that life would then be seen more in terms of transactions and institutions in which no reference to the divine is made. Secularity, as a concept, then gradually became a system of social ethics based upon a doctrine which posited the precept that it should not be based on religion and, to them, this new view of religion is responsible for the most momentous of the intellectual changes which brought about modern consciousness.

From the 18th - 19th century, Christians nearly all over Europe, accepted the concept of secularization in the full belief that the teachings of Christ can only be fully understood through the day to day worldly affairs of man. If this broad and liberal view of secularism were accepted by the critics of Sharia and were allowed to form the basis upon which the concept of a secular state rests, then the grounds for the fear of Nigeria joining any particular international organization would appear to have no foundation whatsoever. The arguments against both the membership of the OIC and operation of Sharia will then appear to be more of a political imbroglio cast in the umbra of religion rather than any cogent or far-reaching argument. F. C. Ruxton, a British Colonial Officer in Nigeria, in the introduction to his book, Maliki Law, explains the position of Nigerian Muslims succinctly. He observes:

> Muhammadan (read Islamic) Law in all its detail, religious as well as civil, has for us an immense interest. It necessitates the study of the social institutions of a people which an immutable law has for twelve and half centuries, moulded and remoulded at frequent intervals. For here it has been neither the nation nor the people which has made the law; it is the law which has and moulded the nation and people ... In Islam there is but one law there is but the law and that is signified in the word Sharia.

Ruxton is, to a large extent, correct in his assessment of the view of the Muslim to their law. For the Muslim he sees the law as a dogma. What is often ignored is that, to St Augustine and St Aquinas, the founders of modern law, the law was also dogma. St Augustine defined the relations between the Church and State but did not see the need to separate them. To him, like most modern theologians, civil law, the law of daily conduct in social life, must be dominated and inspired by religious thought or principles.

Common Law as it developed in Europe can be discussed in a variety of senses. First, Scruton defines the term by two contrasts - namely Common Law versus Equity and Common Law versus Statute. In the first contrast, Common Law is seen as a part of the law in which legal remedies are determined and sought on the basis of a definite breach of law, whereas remedies in equity are available even in the absence of any breach of law. In the second contrast, Common Law is defined through judicial decisions as opposed to law laid down through legislative processes. In the second sense, Common Law can be overridden by equity. In the third sense, Common Law in continental Europe, notably France and Germany, denotes law common to an entire political entity as opposed to only a section of it.

To Muslims, Islamic Law emanates from God and all other law is of human origin and can be changed or modified because it emanates from temporal authority. It is important to note that early Christian theologians (notably St Augustine and St Aquinas) held the same view of Christian law. *The True Law*, to them, is eternal or divine law, and positive law is human law designed to supplement divine law and to mankind's temporal needs. The idea of supremacy of Common Law is an outgrowth of the concept of secularity. The Muslims tend to question this sense of supremacy. They argue that supremacy of Common Law had been established on the grounds of its divine source, then the idea may not have been questioned. However, history tells us that the idea of the supremacy of Common Law emanated from an incident involving a Chief Justice of England, Justice Tresillian. The close association of the English judges with the royalty at times necessarily involved them in political crises. Keeton recalls that English judges were deeply involved in the constitutional upheavals of King Richard Ifs reign. The prolonged struggle ended in the execution of Chief Justice Tresillian after he was found guilty of an alleged treason while in his judicial capacity. He was arrested during his trial and hanged. This incident was a harsh lesson for the English judges. The incident gradually led to the development of the concept of "judicial neutrality" and with it the principle of judicial independence.

Chief Justice Markham and Sir John Fortescue were in the forefront of the struggle for the independence of English judiciary. During the wars of the Roses, the two judges declined to bend the law to suit royal policies. In a celebrated treatise for the education of Prince Edward (1471), Fortescue described England as a limited constitutional monarchy and asserted that "Common law is supreme and even the sovereign must observe it". It follows that if the relations of the judges with royalty had remained cordial, Common Law may never have been declared as supreme. There is no gainsaying that the concept of a supremacy of the common law is most beneficial to the ordinary citizen in that it gives him the benefit of equality, but the fact remains that its assumption of that status was incidental not natural.

The Muslims argue that the supremacy of law has its roots in its divine nature and, because the Qur'an has maintained its originality, this nature has not changed. The Islamic concept of equality of all litigants before the law, which gives practical expression to the idea of supremacy of law was elucidated by Prophet Muhammad (SAW) in his advice to judges:

> "Let the hudud of Allah be applied equally on your relatives and the total strangers. You should not care a bit for the reproachment of any critic whatsoever." (A.R.I. Doi, Shana, p. 12)

The Muslim case against the use of the word supreme when referring to common law appears weak because what is Important ultimately in the recognition of the law is considered to be supreme, the circumstances notwithstanding.

The validity of the suggestion that secularity enhances progress because it does not encumber human free will has remained questionable. Both Japan and Turkey hold a somewhat different view of secularity from the West and yet they have made enviable progress in their development. The Japanese concepts of secularity, for example, is imbedded in Shintoism and Buddhism. If secularity has any place in Nigeria and the freedom of choice in religion is to be maintained in the society, then the choice is clear; each to his own and yet in harmony. After all, there is no threat to one from the other.

Non-Muslims may find it interesting to know that a recent analysis of the contents of the Qur'an, classifies the substance of its teaching into two broad categories. First the spiritual aspect which covers knowledge about God, about His prophets, the aims of religion, the angels and their functions, about man himself and the Day of Judgement. The second deals with the all embracing nature of Islam as it attempts to help mankind to achieve peace, happiness and prosperity in this world. The analysis reveals that most of the surahs revealed in Mecca are about the spiritual aspects of life while most of those revealed in Medina deal with the social and political aspects of life.

Imam Rashid Husain, in his book *Quranology*, attempts a classification of the Medinan surahs in modern perspective. He outlines them as follows:

1. Surah al-Baqara - Political constitution
2. Surahs al-Imran al-Azhab and al-Bayinah - Religious Education
3. Surah-an-Nisa and al-Talaq - Social welfare and matrimonial affairs
4. Surah al-Ma'idah - Health service

5. Surahs al-Anfal, at-Taubah and al-Mumtahana - Defence, War and Refugees
6. Surahs al-Hajj and al-Hujurat - Foreign Affairs and Unity of Nations
7. Surah an-Nur - Justice
8. Surahs al-Hadid, al-Fath and at-Tagabun - Finance, Revenue and Monetary Policy
9. Surah al-Mujadalah - Internal Affairs
10. Surah Muhammad - Labour
11. Surah al-Hashir - Housing
12. Surah al-Tahrim, al-Insan and al-Zilzal - Fuel, Power, Water and Atomic Energy
13. Surah al-Jumua - Trade
14. Surah al-Munafiqun - Land and Natural Resources
15. Surah al-As-Saff - Information and Communication. The Encyclopaedia Americana (vol XVI, p. 412) attempts a similar broad classification of the substance of the Qur'an into two spheres of life - namely (1) the spiritual (religious) and (2) secular (comprising political, economic, social and cultural aspects of life). The Western mind is critical of Islam on the grounds that its system controls all the varied domains of human activity. In other words, the focal point of attention of the critics is the seemingly inseparable nature of the religious, political and social aspects of the affairs of an Islamic society. What they fail to foresee is the tragic consequences of lack of effective control on the passions of mankind in his social and political activities in a world dominated by extreme individualism and selfishness. Hobbes insists that it is inherent in human nature not to be satisfied with what one possesses. Mankind is today capable of obliterating from this earth, in a matter of seconds the civilization we know today in an attempt to promote his own selfish interest. In his book, *1999*, former American President Richard Nixon, confirmed this

imminent threat when he predicted that the choice for mankind in the year 2,000 is between better future and survival to enjoy the future. He reminded us that in the year 1000 religious leaders, guided by Biblical prophecy, predicted the destruction of the earth by God's power, but in the year 2,000 the prediction assumes a different dimension - it is the destruction of the earth by human power "unleashing the power of the atom." Nixon stopped short of asking a rhetorical question - how do we avert this danger in a practical manner?

It is interesting to note that Napoleon Bonaparte, the 19th Century Emperor of France, seems to have foreseen the need for the normative control of human behaviour when he observes with approbation:

> I hope the time is not far off when I shall be able to unite all the wise and educated men of all the countries and establish a uniform regime based on the principles of the Qur'an which alone are true and which alone can lead men to happiness. (Bonaparte et Islam by Cherfils, Paris, France 227, pp. 105-125)

Napoleon was alleged to be hypocritical about his views on Islam because of his hidden desire to conquer Egypt. It is worthy of note, however, that he did perceive the need for a radical change at the time. However, Sir Bernard Shaw, a highly respected 20th Century English Christian intellectual, seems genuinely to be in complete agreement with Napoleon when he opines:

> I have prophesied about the faith of Muhammad, that it would be acceptable to Europe of today. Medieval ecclesiastics either through ignorance or bigotry, painted Islam in the darkest colours. They were in fact trained to hate both the man Muhammad and his religion. To them Muhammad was anti-Christ. I have studied him, the wonderful man (Muhammad) and in my opinion far from being anti-Christ must be called the saviour of humanity. I believe that if a man like him were to

> assume the leadership of the modem world, he would succeed in solving the problems in a way that would bring it to the much needed peace and happiness. (A History of Intellectual Development of Europe, London, 1875, by J. W. Drapar, pp. 329- 330)

Reverend J. M. Rodwell was courageous enough to express an honest opinion which is worth noting. It is one which most non-Muslims would prefer to keep to themselves. He observes:

> It must be acknowledged, too that the Koran (Qur'an) deserves the highest praise for its conceptions of Divine nature, in reference to the attributes of Power, Knowledge and Universal Providence and Unity that its belief and trust in the One God of Heaven and Earth is deep and fervent and that... it embodies most of a noble and deep moral earnestness and sententious oracular wisdom, and has proved that there are elements in it on which mighty nations and empires can be built up (Quranology p. 193)

The central theme of these strong views is that humanity ought not be sacrificed on the altar of secularity in the name of progress. The views suggest that progress is attainable at any level without the aid of the concept of secularity.

CHAPTER 8

CANON LAW AS A SYSTEM OF LAW

Attempts have been made to compare Sharia with Canon law. However, there appears to be no basis for the comparison of the two legal systems. Although it would be true to say that both Sharia and Canon law have a strong religious connotation, they actually have little else in common.

Canon Law has had a long history of development throughout Christian history. It is not a static body of laws in that it reflects both social and ecclesiastical changes of the past. Canon law as we know it today is the product of the determined efforts of Pope Gregory VII (who reigned from 1073 - 85) to win independence for the Church from the existing systems of private Churches and to diminish papal dependence on the Roman nobility and their Emperor. Canon Law was designed, therefore, as an intrinsic part of a centralized religious system such as the Church.

Islam is not centralized in its system of organization and, as such, does not require the equivalent of Canon law. Sharia, as stated earlier, is a full system of law which deals with every aspect of law, both civil and criminal. This cannot be said of Canon law (see Richard Hooker's *Laws of Ecclesiastical Polity*). Indeed although, in its wider sense, Canon law does include the precepts of divine, natural and positive law which have been incorporated into its code, it essentially remains a body of laws and regulations governing the behaviour of individuals and institutions operating solely within the Church system. Indeed, Canon law effectively functioned in different periods in the history of the organization of the Church and, in actual fact, played a major role in the reception and transmission of Common Law (Greek and Roman jurisprudence) throughout Christendom. As Islam does not have a centralized institution such as the Church to which it turns for practical guidance in matters of religion, there is no need for Muslims to have a set regulations such as Canon law. In essence, Canon Law can be seen, in the simplest terms, as a set of regulations which guide the internal functions of the institutions of the Roman Catholic Church.

Chapter 9

BRITISH APPROACH TO SHARIA IN NIGERIA

Muslims, all over the world, operated a definite legal system governing all aspects of their life, transactions (public and private) and international dealings. The European powers, notably the British, the French and the Dutch, were faced with the problem of having to impose their laws on the countries they colonized or accept the local laws in the governance of those territories. In most cases, they had to use a combination of both laws, but with the European laws having an upper hand. It is of special interest to us to know how the British handled their case in Nigeria. The combined irresistible influence of Britain, France, Germany and Italy, after the partition of Africa (1885-1902) imposed the European legal systems on the Maghrib, Morocco, Tunisia and Nigeria in West Africa. A. R. I. Doi, in his book *Sharia the Islamic Law*, summed up the views of the colonialists on Sharia as a legal system. He quoted Lord Macaulay in India as saying that the "Islamic legal system was outmoded and did not provide any justice whatsoever" and Lord Lugard in Nigeria as saying that the "Sharia system was repugnant to natural justice and humanity". Students from these countries who studied in European institutions later participated in shaping the hybrid legal system called Anglo-"Muhammedan" or Franco-"Muhammedan" law. It was a compromise plan to appease the Muslims and was achieved only after a long and arduous process of change.

The initial impact of Common Law or the European legal system on Muslim societies was felt first in the area of public law, then in inter constitutional and criminal law. By the time most of these societies became independent their civil and commercial transactions had been europeanised. The colonialists were careful enough not to insist on radical changes in the personal law of the Muslims because of its direct impact on the life of the people and its sensitive nature. The first to be influenced by the Europeans legal system was the Ottoman Caliphate, the most powerful Muslim power, following its capitulation in the 19th Century. The system was first introduced under the guise of protecting the interest of Europeans living in the Middle East as traders and civil servants. The Ottomans introduced the first series of reforms of their legal system, known as *Tan'zimat*, between 1839 and 1876. By 1850 the French commercial code was accepted in full in place of Sharia. In *1858*, the Ottomans adopted the French penal code to replace the provisions of Sharia. In 1875 Egypt also adopted the French penal law to replace some aspects of Sharia.

Countries like Turkey whose modernization have been attributed to their secularization cannot divest themselves totally of the religious context of their original legal systems. The persistent element of Islamic influence in Turkish society prevents Turkey from being fully accepted in the European Community. More than a few times, she has been referred to as the "sick man" of Europe.

The British were faced with the problem of what to do with Sharia in Nigeria. In 1909 when they were planning to amalgamate the Northern and Southern protectorates of Nigeria into a single political entity under one central government. Sharia was central in their decision. The question then was how to unite the two systems of law which operate in the two protectorates? They had two choices open to them. First, to abolish Sharia unilaterally and impose Christian law all over the country. Second, to allow the two systems to coexist in the hope that experience would provide the necessary ingredients to effect the inevitable structural modification in the systems to make for peace and progress in the country. They chose the second option.

The problem Nigeria has today in the field of law stems from the fact that British have left, but they have also left behind them a biased view of the Sharia system. Too many of the non-Muslims in the colonized societies have inherited those European prejudices against Islam. The Europeans knew nothing or very little about Islam and the "principles" upon which its legal system is based, yet they were quick to condemn it as "unprogressive", "impracticable", "out-moded" and "unenlightened" as compared to their own religion and its legal system. What most non- Muslims in the former European colonies ignore, whenever Sharia is discussed, is that its condemnation by the colonialists was part of their grand design to colonize them mentally as well as physically. Experience has since then proved that it was part of a deliberate plan to destroy anything good of ours including our political, social and legal systems and to implant and perpetuate their own, and in most cases to the detriment of future peace and stability in the development of those nations.

When we approach the whole issue objectively, we will discover that the grounds upon which the case against Sharia are based are very weak since the sources of both Common Law and Sharia are the sacred books - the Holy Bible and the Holy Qur'an. Each of the two sources is considered as divine by Christians and Muslims respectively. The great theologians of both faiths were, in early times, identified with the task of defining justice and the principles upon which its administration ought to be based. The differences between the two legal systems that emanated from the two different sets of legal principles were clearly due to different interpretations of God's injunctions by subsequent jurists and theologians. Over the centuries, the Sharia and Common Law systems have worked side by side before independence in many of the countries colonized by European powers. Conflicts have arisen as a result of their operation but this is to be expected. Even in the same legal system operating in different nations conflict of law is known to exist. However, experience has shown that, in the operation of Common Law and Sharia in the same society, while co-existence is possible fusion is not. The conflicts that have arisen can be minimized to a degree where peaceful coexistence can be guaranteed and maintained.

The impression being given about Sharia is that it is too rigid and harsh. This view of Sharia is very misleading. The divine injunctions which form its basis are clearly defined in the Qur'an and Sunnah. The principles upon which Islamic justice is based are well established by the founders of the four Islamic schools of thought and jurisprudence. Doi believes, and his view is shared by many, that if the process of Ijma, Qyiyas, Masalih al-Mursalah, Istislah and Istidlal are followed carefully and conscientiously, Sharia can meet the inevitable challenges of modernization and everchanging necessities of modern life.

As indicated earlier, the frequent criticism leveled against Sharia is the apparent harshness and rigidity of some of its edicts. Non-Muslims feel that it is morally repugnant and somewhat uncivilized to cut off the hand of a thief. The facts of the matter are that the adherence to such penal codes in the Sharia system of law is not effected in any Muslim society save that of Saudi Arabia. It is felt that as Saudi Arabia is the birth place of the Islamic religion and, therefore remains the modern centre of its influence, it is understandable that its application of a Sharia Law ought to reflect as much originality as possible. The fact that rigid adherence to the Roman Catholic interpretation of Christian Law makes for a strict regime of discipline in the Holy See due to its position as the centre of influence for Catholicism is equally understandable. However, neither of these extreme examples should form the basis for the assessment of the respective systems of law in those states.

The fact that Roman Catholics abhor the concepts of divorce, abortion or contraception is merely the result of their rigid interpretation and application of God's injunctions in Christian Law regarding the sanctity of marriage, the inalienability of the right to life and the pre-eminence of the divine process of creation. These areas of belief do not necessarily project or diminish the stature of the faith of which they are a part and they certainly do not validate or invalidate Christianity of its concomitant social and legal constitutions. They are merely the practical interpretations of one section of Christendom of certain parts of the divine injunctions that distinguish their way of life from those of other persuasions.

Those who acknowledge a dislike of sin find it hard to explain the reason for the enormous disproportion in the evidence of sin in comparisons conducted between Muslim and Christian societies. The purist Muslim may well see fit to have a habitual thief dismembered for his crime. What, however, is the harm in having a powerful legal disincentive for crime (or sin) when such a disincentive is so effective in its deterrence that it is hardly ever used. In other words, a disproportionately greater number of thieves are fined and jailed in a comparable non-Muslim society than those who have their hands amputated in Saudi Arabia. Ironically, the crime of theft, which is reviled by all religions, appears to have no remedy in the former while it appears to be effectively under control in the latter. Curiously, even in Muslim societies where penal Sharia is not enforced, the level of almost all crimes (sins) in the society are startlingly lower than those to be found in comparable non-Muslim societies. The question becomes: which is preferable; a "civilized" society with a so-called modern system of operation which appears to have no remedy to rampant spiralling crime (sin) or a supposedly "uncivilized" society with a seemingly archaic system of operation which is evidently successful in maintaining a relatively crime (and sin) free society? The answer to this question is personal preference 'and freedom of choice. in different ways, the Vatican is as repressive and dogmatic as Medina and Casablanca as liberal and *lassiez-faire* as the Costa Brava. So, therefore, each to his own with no recriminations. That is the way forward.

Table I indicates the present state of Islamic personal law in the

Muslim world. In most of the countries the law has remained unchanged and uncodified.

Table 1

Country	*Muslims in the Country*	*Present State of islamic family law*
Afghanistan	Overwhelming majority	unchanged and uncodilied
Bahrain	Overwhelming majority	unchanged and uncodified
lIunna	minority	" "
Ethiopia	minority	" "
Gambia	majority	" "
Ghana	minority	" "
Kuwait	overwhelming majority	
Libya		slightly modified and codified
Maldive	' "	unchanged and uncodified
Mali majority	" "	
Mauritani	overwhelming majority	" "
Nigeria	majority '	" "
Gatar	effectively 100% Muslims	" "
Saudi Arabia	" "	
Sieira Lcoii	minority	" "
Somalia	overwhelming majority	" "
Yemen	" "	"
Yugoslavia	minority	slightly changed but uncodified

See Tahic Mahmood, "Family Law Reform in the World' - New Delhi 1972, pp. 270-272.

Table 2 shows the countries where the Sharia has been changed through modern legislative process, thus subjecting the Islamic Institution to regulatory measures. Muslims and Christian scholars have described these changes as "Law Reforms".

Table 2

Country	*Years of Reform*
Ceylon 1951	The Aspect of Muslim Law Already Changed and Codified
Algeria 1959	Consent of parties to marriage, solenmization of marriage, divorce, rights of children
Bninei 1955	Betrothal, marriage, divorce, maintenance, matrimonial offences
Ceylon 1951	Registration of marriage, marriage-age for women, guardianship, bigamy, divorce by husband, dissolution of marriage by court.
Egypt 1920,23,29	Marriage-age, women's rights, divorce, Iddah' period of gestation, custody of children matrimonial disputes and some aspects of the law of inheritance and bequests.
India 1929,37,39	Dissolution of women's marriage, by court, (the whole of India) registration of marriage, amount of dowry, 1876, 1920, 1935, marriage age, gestation, effect of apostasy on 1942 (particular states) marriage and inheritance.
Indonesia 1946,47,55	Registration of marriage, marriage-age, divorce by husband, delegated divorce.
Iran 1931, 37, 48,67	Some aspects of the law of marriage and divorce
Iraq 1959,63	Bigamy, marriage-contract, maintenance, divorce by husband, dissolution of marriage by court
Jordan 1951	Some aspects of the law of marriage and divorce
Lebanon	Some aspects of the law of marriage and divorce
Malaysia 1949 to 1964	Betrothal, guardianship in marriage, registration of marriage, divorce by husband, delegated divorce bigamy, dissolution of marriage by court, family disputes, matrimonial offences.
Morocco 1957 to 1958	Some aspects of the law of marriage and divorce, including bigamy; dissolution of women's marriage by court; some aspects of the law of intestate and testimony succession, including orphaned grandchildren's right to inheritance.
Nigeria 1955	Adopted Penal Code which transferred criminal law to the Common Law Court.
Pakistan 1961 to 1962	Registration of marriage, effect of apostasy on marriage and inheritance, divorce by husband,

	bigamy, dissolution of women's marriage by court, orphaned grand children's right to inheritance, life estates.
Singapore 1957to 1960	As in Malaysia and Brunei.
Sudan 1916 to 1960	Guardianship-in-marriage, divorce by husband, dissolution of women's marriage by court, period of gestation, spouse-relict's rights to inheritance, some special cases of inheritance, bequest to heirs.
Syria 1953	Some aspects of the laws relating to marriage, divorce, inheritance and bequest.
Tunisia 1956	Some aspects of the laws relating to marriage, divorce, inheritance and bequest.

The British did not have a ready answer to the complex Sharia problem which confronted them when they colonized Nigeria. It occurred to them that the French had faced an identical problem when they occupied Algeria. Both Nigerian and Algerian Muslims are followers of the Maliki school of law. In order to find a practical solution to this problem, the French commissioned the complete translation of the Mukhtasar compendium of Sidi Khalil of the Maliki school of thought. The work was carried out in 1848 by Dr Perron under the supervision of the French Government. The complete work consisted of 6 volumes and a one volume index (3, 858 pages). In addition to this work the French requested a Turkish diplomatist, Ambassador Savvas Pasha, to give a lecture on the advisability of substituting French law for the native law (Sharia) in their colonies. The talk was under the auspices of the Societe des Etudes Coloniales (Society for Colonial Studies). The lecture was delivered in Paris on the 28th of January 1892. The summary of the recommendations on how to handle the Muslims and their law made by the Turkish diplomatist was:

(a) Their personal status should never be touched by the governing power. There should be no appeal in these matters to Government Courts.

(b) The Islamic Forum should be re-introduced: the Judge (Khadi); the juri-consul-praetor (Mufti), he who assists the Khadi and expounds the law, supplying him with fatawa or decisions; the court of doctrinal counsel, Bab al-fatawa.

(c) Criminal cases should on no account be left to any other than the Government Courts (the writer was unaware that Muslims worship God and not Mohammed (PBUH). Should Muhammedans (read Muslims) not like the Criminal Law of the Christians, all they have to do is not to commit crimes.

(e) In the time, commercial cases will have to be tried in the Government Courts. Justice, apart from the personal status of Muhanimedans (read Muslims), must be one and the same for all. Before this can be realized, our law must be Islamized. By this is meant the process of rendering the rules of law of the Governing Power conformable to the juridical concepts of Islam, by demonstrating that they are not contrary to the fundamental principles of Muhammadan (read Islamic) Law and that their introduction is called for by the needs of the age. The Prophet himself foresaw the need for modification. Adoption is thus allowable, even recommended; it must, however, be done in conformity with the methods of Islam, its orthodox rules and procedure ... One last recommendation: study well Muhammadan (read Islamic) Law. If their Law is not thoroughly well known and understood, Muhammedans (read Muslims) can only be governed by physical force.

As best we know, the British left Sharia alone in Nigeria and, a few years before independence they engineered the acceptance of item (c) of Ambassador Pasha's ideas following a recommendation by a panel of legal experts (three of whom were British).

Muslim scholars continue to question the validity of the theoretical idea behind the concept of the secular state and opine that they are fraught with the danger of unwittingly drifting away from the control of divine injunctions towards a situation of self-destruction, all in the name of progress. This fear was shared by early Christians when, in the wake of the Reformation, the concepts of secularism and secularity, emerged and posed a serious threat to the unity of the Church. In his comments on Machiavelli, J. R. Hale observed that Machiavelli's secular approach to politics was as late as the 16th Century considered scandalous because it was inconsistent with the Church's view of state and its affairs. The term Machiavellism has to this day a stigma of immorality attached to it. Their fear then was, to some extent, justified because as a consequence the material interests of mankind have tended to override all other interests, religious or otherwise. By implication, mankind is gradually drifting back to his original 'state of nature', in which he is his own worst enemy.

The greatest problem Sharia faces, as a legal system, is the allegation against it that it is a barbaric, impracticable and unprogressive system because of its seemingly static nature. The critics of Islam see Sharia as an impediment to modernization. Ironically, it was Muslim Spain under Sharia which recorded monumental achievements in the establishment of excellent and enduring educational institutions that was to become the bedrock of modern science and technology. There is ample evidence to suggest that Islamic law, like Common law, can develop and take care of unforeseen circumstances as the society in which it operates changes. These allegations are therefore mere propaganda unrelated to reality. The allegations seems to be designed to confuse the minds of the Nigerian populace. The static image which is painted of Islamic law had its roots in the mistaken but widely accepted belief that research in Islamic jurisprudence had ended with the four orthodox founders of the schools of Islamic law. This led to the development of the somewhat misleading concept of *Taqlid* which means rigid adherence to the school of thought to which one originally belonged. This idea had the effect of retarding progress in the development of the Islamic legal system capable of meeting the needs of changing societies. However the amazing scientific phenomena predicted in the Qur'an a century and a half ago which are now being proven by modern science and technology is sufficient indication that the era of belief in the limits in the field of knowledge was one of short-sighted folly. With the gradual but unforeseen transformation of the world into what one can properly describe as 'a large village', the followers of the four schools of Islamic jurisprudence (Hanifah, Shafi'i. Maliki and Hanbal) now find it imperative to be in contact with one another more often than was ever imagined at the time the orthodox schools of legal thought were founded. This unforeseen development in human communication has paved the way for the development of the concept of *Takhayyur* which denotes freedom of choice. This concept seems to provide the answer to the conflict of laws in the four schools. Today, there is hardly any clear demarcation of the areas where one particular school is predominant. The doctrine of Takhayyur had existed right from the advent of Islam. During the time of the Prophet Muhammad (PBUH) and the 'Tabi'un' who came after him, it was seen as mere difference of opinions among the Ummah. Doi reminds us that it was the need to accommodate each other's points of view which led to the development of *Takhayyur* as a concept. If its development is handled properly, it can enhance progress in the modem world. Qadis may find difficulties in app1ying freely the principles of this new concept. Some scholars have attempted to convince them that their freedom to apply the principles is not in conflict with the idea of the founders of the fiqh schools. On the contrary, such an act could enhance the development of a harmonious process for the administration of justice. Scholars further argued that *Takhayyur* which leads to *Talfiq* (fusion of juristic opinions) is not a deviation from the spirit of Qur'an or Sunnah. To some Islamic scholars the reinterpretation of Islamic legal principles through Takhayyur and Talfiq to meet the needs of our ever changing social circumstances is interpreted as a deviation from the well established principles of justice. This is not necessarily so. What is objectionable is the mere importation of the substance of alien legal systems into the Islamic system, in particular where there is a clear conflict of laws. This type of indiscriminate importation often described as *neo-Ijti* had can lead to deviation from the original divine injunctions. The idea of deviation from established principles applies to the Christian legal system as well. As indicated elsewhere in this work, in spite of all the advantages that modem family planning offers, I the Vatican sees abortion as an unlawful termination of life, purely and simple. In other words, the idea is in sharp conflict with divine injunction - "Thou shall not kill". The Vatican also does not recognize divorce on the grounds that it is in conflict with another divine injunction - "No one must put asunder what God has put together". However, in recognition of the wider implication of human behaviour, the Vatican allows what is called a "legal separation" (a period of possible reconciliation when a couple may choose to reunite).

Having briefly discussed Islamic law and some of its future potentials, one can safely say that it is neither static nor unprogressive in that the system is capable of adapting itself to the ever changing conditions of mankind. The progressive nature of Islam and evidently its legal system is confirmed by Sir Bernard Shaw when he observes:

> I have always held the religion of Muhammad in high estimation because of its wonderful vitality. It is the only religion which appears to possess the assimilating capacity to changing phases of existence which can make itself appeal to all ages...

Implied in the application of the concepts of *Takhayyur* and *Talflq* is the need for the Qadis and scholars involved to exercise great care in their analysis of the potentials of the law. Those involved must be of proven ability, knowledge,. maturity and above all deep conviction in the Islamic faith (Taqwah). It is the only way to allay the fears of those who see, in any attempt to reinterpret the established principles of Islamic Law or any law for that matter, a major deviation from the tenets of the religion.

Even though, the British have accepted those of Ruxton's recommendations on Sharia that indicate it would be unwise to abolish the system in Nigeria, it later became evident that the acceptance was qualified. The Grand Qadi of Bauchi State, Abdulmalik Bappa Mahmud, draws attention to the deliberate, systematic and determined efforts by the successive British Colonial administrations in Nigeria to undermine the operation of the Sharia System. First, Lord Lugard withdrew the recognition of all Sharia Courts and in 1904 and established 8 courts with limited powers for the whole of Northern Nigeria. This was followed by the *Native Courts Proclamation Ordinance* of 1906. On the surface the courts appeared to have wide powers, but in reality their judicial powers were severely curtailed in their jurisdiction. The courts were graded into five categories with the Emir's Courts given jurisdiction over homicide cases. Justice Mahmud asserts that what the *Provincial Courts Proclamation Ordinance* of 1906 established were in reality English Courts and it conferred on the Resident "the power of a superior judge with unlimited powers". Under this arrangement, the Resident could delegate judicial powers to Divisional Officers to serve as judges, magistrates or assessors.

It was at this stage that judges were brought from. England to man the Magistrate Courts, High Courts and Supreme Court and they brought English laws with them.

The Native Court Ordinance was, in effect, a scheme designed to set in motion the processes of final destruction of the Sharia System in Nigeria. It was introduced on the eve of the amalgamation of Nigeria in 1914. Section (2) of the Ordinance provides that "Native Law includes Islamic Law". This relegates Sharia to an inferior position relative to Customary Law. Subsequent reviews of the Ordinance led to the acceptance of the Brooke Commission's recommendations which resulted in the reenactment of the Native Courts Law of 1956 and, finally, the Area Courts Edict of 1968. The Edict prevented the Area Courts from applying any native law and custom which is inconsistent with "natural justice, equity and good conscience". Justice Mahmud asserts that the High Courts were empowered to nullify decisions of the Native Courts which failed the "repugnancy test". The criteria for the test was simply consistency with the substance of English Law. Mixed courts were established in the Sabon Garis to try non- indigenes on the grounds of religion or local custom.

In Lugard's time the deliberate dislocation between the English legal system and the Sharia system even went to the extent of separating prisoners according to the type of court that convicted them. There would appear to be other logic to this other than to create an artificial distinction between the two forms of justice dispensed rather than the nature of the crimes committed which is the normal criterion. The establishment of separate prisons for convicts of Sharia Courts and those of the Magistrates Courts is a clear indication of the attitude of circumspection adopted by the British colonizers towards the Sharia system.

In his book *A Brief History of Sharia in the Defunct Northern Nigeria*, Hon. Justice Mahmud, identifies a number of classical cases (*Mariyama Vs Sadiku Ejo* (1961), N.R.N.L.R. 81 (*Abba Vs Mary T. Baikie* K/20A/1943, *Dawudu Vs Danmole*, I.W.L.R. 1053 1962, *Gun Vs Hadeja* N.A.H.F.S.C 1959, and *Bangbose Vs Daniel*, 14 W.A.C.A. 1952) to illustrate the high- handed manner in which English Courts reversed the decisions of Native Courts ostensibly on the grounds that the decisions were made on law which is alleged to be repugnant to "natural justice, equity and good conscience". In his book, Islamic Survey: A History of Islamic Law, Coulson Highlighted the British prejudice against Islamic Law when he questioned the right of the Muslims to formulate their laws in Arab countries, Spain and Morocco and then introduce them to Nigeria to displace customary laws. Coulson seems to ignore the fact that this is exactly what English law is set out to do in Nigeria, that is to exert its supremacy over all other laws in the country.

In *Maniyama Vs Sadiku Ejo*, for example, the plaintiff sued his divorced wife who remarried before the prescribed period (Idda) of waiting, and begat a child 10 months after the divorce. The Native Court ruled that the child belonged to the plaintiff. The High Court of Northern Nigeria reversed the decision on the grounds that the Igbira custom did not recognize the period of waiting. In *Abba Vs Mary T. Baikie*, a Native Court ruled that Mary being a Christian could not inherit the property of her Muslim father. The Supreme Court reversed this decision on the ground that it was repugnant to natural justice. However, in another case - *Dawodu Vs Danmole*, Dawodu sued to get a share of his deceased father's property which was denied him by the Yoruba custom (Idi Igi) because his mother was not in the house when the father died. All the higher courts upheld that decision because it was consistent with the local custom even though it was clearly against natural justice. Here English Law was not deliberately used as the criteria.

In *Gun Vs Hadeja* N.A., the Emir's Court found Gun guilty of robbery and homicide and sentenced him to death, but the Federal Supreme Court reversed the decision on the grounds that the rule of procedure and evidence of Islamic Law was repugnant to natural justice. In *Gubba Vs Gwandu* N.A., the Emir's Court found the defendant guilty of murder of a person he found having an affair with his wife and sentenced him to death. The decision was reversed on the grounds that under English Law, a death sentence would not have been passed on a person who acted under a situation of extreme provocation. However, in *Katsina N.A. Vs Abakillahi Kogo* in which the Emir's Court found the defendant guilty of homicide, on appeal to the West African Court of Appeal (W.A.C.A) the decision was upheld and returned to Katsina Native Authority (N.A.) even though there was no admission of guilt, witness or any evidence to prove that the crime was committed by the defendant. Under English Law, the death sentence would not have been passed on the defendant. Another interesting case which is a glaring example of prejudice against Islamic Law was *Yunusa Rasaq Vs Titi* (1968, N.N.C.R. 97) in which a Yoruba Muslim before his death bequeathed his property to one of his children to the exclusion of the others. The High Court of Northern Nigeria held that the will could not be relied upon because it was against the interest of the deceased's other Muslim children. On appeal, the Supreme Court overruled the decision of the High Court on the grounds that its decision was contrary to the English Wills Act of 1837 which allows anybody to dispose of his property to any one he wishes, even to his dog. Is this really consistent with natural justice?

It is evident from these examples given that the British went all out to establish the supremacy of English Law over Islamic Law and even went to the ridiculous extent of classifying Islamic Law, which is a written law, below customary ones. The surreptitious inclusion of Sharia Courts in the agenda of the 1958 London Constitutional Conference was the culmination of years of British prejudice and determined effort to undermine the Sharia system. The issue came up at the London Conference to the surprise of many Muslim members of the Nigerian delegation but readily supported by others. The Muslim members fearing that they might be blackmailed again over the issue of independence, compromised and the motion was adopted. The resolution proposed that "No person shall be tried for a criminal offence except for an offence which is codified under a written law". This provision was adopted in the 1960 Constitution. Since then, the provisions of subsequent Nigerian Constitution seem to have been drafted in such a manner as to provide deliberate loopholes to frustrate the implementations of Islamic Law. This is evident in the series of challenges to the constitutional provisions and laws enacted since independence. (see appendix IV).

There is sufficient evidence in the history of the development of Islamic Law in Nigeria from the advent of British administration to date to suggest that the problems the system faces are of political nature and not religious. First, the British have no fear of being Islamized. This applies also to the Nigerian non-Muslims. This must be so because there is no compulsion or missionary culture in Islam. Evidence of political motives are manifest in the decision of the National Council of Nigeria and Cameroons (NCNC) to agree to support an amendment of the 1960 Constitution to pave the way for the removal of the legal obstacles in the High Court Law which frustrated the work of the High Court of the North. The compromise agreement reached with the NCNC was on condition that they, too, would first be supported by the Northern Peoples Congress (NPC) on a certain matter they were interested. One does not compromise on matters of faith like religion.

The conflicting position of Nigerian legal experts and political leaders over the years on the establishment of a Federal Sharia Court of Appeal is a clear indication that political motives rather than religious ones are the main obstacles in the way to finding lasting solution to the problem. Chief Ezeife, a member of the second Constituent Assembly, was honest enough to admit in a newspaper contribution to the debate on the issue that the problem with Sharia is not religious. The importance of his contribution is that the Sharia issue is simply a matter of give and take, in political not religious terms.

What is imperative in our development as a people is the recognition of the fact that law is the expression of the norms, mores and values of a people. In short, it is the embodiment of that which a society values above all else in the lives its acknowledged "soul" of a people. It follows logically that in the development of a society nothing should endanger its soul. American action in Japan during the second world war is worth noting when the American Commanding Officers was selecting his targets for the nuclear bombing of Japanese cities, he was well advised to exclude the city of Kyoto, the heart of the Japanese culture. American experts argued that since Kyoto is, in cultural terms, the soul of Japan it would defeat the purpose of war it is were destroyed. It was concluded that the purpose of war is to compel people to submission rather than to destroy them completely hence Kyoto city was saved from destruction.

CHAPTER 10

CONCLUSIONS: STABILITY IN A MULTI-RELIGIOUS SOCIETY

If, in spite of the manifestly religious background of Common Law, some Nigerians feel they are justified in actively seeking to have Sharia expunged from the Nigerian Constitution, the question may well be asked - what is to prevent other groups from also seeking to have Common Law expunged on the same grounds? After all there is clear evidence that both systems have deep religious foundations. The issue is not as simple as it appears to be. It is not simply that of a majority vote in the Assembly or even in the country. It is one of principle which requires deep reflection and a thorough assessment of the wider implications of expunging from the constitution any system of law in a multi-religious society.

Now that the Government of President General Ibrahim Babangida has taken away the jurisdiction of Sharia from the Constituent Assembly, the religious tension the issue raised, which appears to have been really only a facade for political tension, is likely to subside. However, it would be an under-estimation of the situation to assume that it would not resurface at various points in time during the course of future debates at the Assembly or after. Regardless of whatever else may happen during the remaining life of the Assembly or after, a number of pertinent issues have emerged from the Federal Government's latest intervention.

Firstly, it is quite clear that Nigerians do not appear to have not learnt any lesson from the previous Sharia controversy since 1978. Secondly, this current incident is bound to raise some doubts in the minds of the Nigerian public about the ability of the Assembly members to justify the confidence reposed in them. Thirdly, reason, logic and consensus, which seem to have sometimes eluded members of the Assembly during its recent debates have, in the past, and should still prove, in the future, to be the safest and most effective implements in the handling of the delicate political issues that can come to the surface in a multi-ethnic and multi-religious society.

An equally important lesson to be learnt from the Government's intervention in the Assembly's work is the apparent deliberate and calculated lack of effort by Nigerian jurists and intellectuals to address the structural and procedural problems central to the relationship among individuals in a multi-religious society. In societies such as ours, there must be a concerted effort to find ways and means of avoiding conflict in the administration of justice. The principles upon which different legal systems are formulated are difficult, if not impossible, to abruptly negate, but the frameworks and procedures within and with which our courts operate can much more easily be modified to meet the ever changing needs of the our society.

It is about time some serious thought was given to the desirable structural changes needed in the operation of our legal systems. The root cause of this nagging problem in our legal system is our failure to address the key legal issues. Instead we try to find simple political solutions to complex legal problems. That approach will not work. At a time when legal contacts between the different groups of Nigerians is constantly and rapidly expanding, the function of our legal system should surely be to establish a balance between certainty and change. It was in this area of investigation that Dr T. Ellias excelled. It was the good fortune of the Nigerian legal system that it should have attracted an intellectual such as Ellias who saw the need to start serious analytical work on African customary law. His attempts at synthesis were most impressive.. His basic aims were to explore its potentialities and, in particular, to assess its capacity to absorb other legal ideas. This initiative was timely because it came at one of the most crucial periods of our legal history. Unfortunately, Dr

Ellias appears to have been a lone pioneer in that vital intellectual endeavour.

The solution to our problem does not lie in being for or against any legal system but rather in finding out how we can together ensure that the systems coexist peacefully to meet the ever growing needs of Nigerian society. Those who support the idea of expunging Sharia from the Nigerian Constitution, must stop to reflect seriously on the wider implications of such an act. They must endeavour to discover the truth about the origins of both Common Law and Sharia which operate in Nigeria and must also have the courage to impart the same to the Nigerian public. It is only our commitment to truth and to reality that will make it possible for us to develop accurate and appropriate perceptions of our laws and institutions which, will in turn, guide our future actions and decisions.

A hierarchy of legal systems in which one takes precedence over the other is clearly not the most ideal prescription for a multi-religious society like that of Nigeria. Indeed, such a state of affairs is almost certain to be fraught with danger. In the final analysis, equality of the Nigerian legal systems, with each system (Sharia, Common and Customary Laws) being represented up to the highest level, seems to proffer the best hope for a lasting solution to our legal structural problems.

These axe most of the realities of our existence as a people to which we must address ourselves conscientiously. However, to make sense of any effort in that direction, we must first have a cogent theoretical base from which to work. There must be an enterprise of thought to enable us to order the facts of our situation into meaningful contexts. We have reached the point at which our intellectuals and jurists must step in to save the situation before the gap between the views of Christians and Muslims on our legal systems widens to an irreconcilable degree. Action now is vital because, without it, these intransigent problems will not go away.

Such is the case with issues which strike at the very core of human co- existence. One hopes that a badly flawed view of the vital link between religion, law and politics in the Constituent Assembly has brought Nigeria's major aspiration one step closer - unity in diversity.

BIBLIOGRAPHY

1. Abduhmalik B. Mahmud *A Brief History of Sharia in the Defunct Northern Nigeria*; Jos University Press (1988)
2. Abdulmalik B. Mahmud *Supremacy of Islamic Law; Zaria*: Hudahuda Publishing (1988)
3. Adigwe, H (Msgr), *Sharia/Canon/Common and Customary Law Courts* (1988)
4. Adler M.J. and Seymour Cain: *Religion and Theology in Great Idea Programme Book 4*; Encyclopaedia Britannica Inc (1961)
5. Adler, M.J. and Wolff, P. "Philosophy of Law and Jurisprudence," in *Great Ideas Programme Book 5*; *Encyclopaedia Britannica* (1961)
6. Anderson, J.N.D. *Islamic Law in Africa* (Second Edition) London: Frank Cass (1970)
7. Blome, Richard: *History of the Old and New Testament*; Written for King William Ill of England; London: (1701)
8. Cherfils Bonaparte et *Islam*, Paris
9. Common Law in the *New Encyclopaedia Britannica*, Vol 4 (1973-74)
10. Cranston Maurice; Rousseau: *The Social Contract*: Penguin Books(1968)
11. Doi Abdur Rahman I; *Sharia the Islamic Law*; London: Ta Ha Publishers, (1984)
12. Imam Husain Rashid; *Quranology*; London: Ta-Ha Publishers (1987)
13. J. J. Rousseau - *The Social Contract and Discourses* (translated by G. D. H. Cole) Everyinaris Library (1913)
14. Keay, E.A. and Richardson S.S. *Law in Africa*; Lagos: Maxwell African University Press (1966)
15. Keeton, George W. *English Law: The Judicial Contribution*; David and Charles, Newton Abbot (1974)
16. Ozigbo, I.R.A. *An Introduction to the Religion and History of Islam* Enugu: Fourth Dimension Publishers, (1988)
17. "Philosophy of Western Law and Jurisprudence": *Encyclopaedia*

Britannica Vol. 10, London: Encyclopaedia Britannica lnc.(1973-74)

18. Plamnientx John; *Man and Society* Vol. II London: (1963)
19. Ruxton, F. *Malik Law* (Summary of a French Translation of Kukbtasar By Sidi Khalil; (Political Department Government of Nigeria, 1914)
20. Ruxton, F.C. *Maliki Law* Published by the British Colonial Office at the request of the Nigerian Government, London: (1909)
21. Sale, George; *Law and the Koran: The Koran, translated for the British Foreign Secretary, Lord Carteret*; London C. Ackers (1734)
22. Scrutton, Roger, *A Dictionary of Political Thought*; London: The Macmillan Press (1982)
23. The *New Encyclopaedia Britannica*, London (1973-74)
24. Thompson, David ed. *Political Ideas Suffolk*: C.A. Watts (1966)
25. Trevor-Roper, Hugh; *Renaissance Essays*, London: Martin Secker and Warburg (1985)
26. William John, *A History of Intellectual development of Europe*; London; Drapar (1875)

APPENDIX I

The Books of the Bible

The Old Testament Books

Books of Law

1. Genesis
2. Exodus
3. Leviticus
4. Numbers
5. Deuteronomy

Books of History

6. Joshua
7. Judge
8. Ruth
9. Samuel I
10. Samuel II
11. Kings I
12. Kings II
13. Chronicles
14. Chronicles II
15. Ezra
16. Nehemiah
17. Esther

Books of Poetry

18. Job
19. Psalms
20. Proverbs
21. Ecclesiastes
22. Songs of Solomon

Books of Prophecy

23. Isaiah
24. Jeremiah
25. Lamentations
26. Ezekiel
27. Daniel
28. Hosea
29. Joel
30. Amos
31. Obadiah
32. Jonah
33. Micah
34. Nahum
35. Habakkuk
36. Zephaniah
37. Haggai
38. Zachariah
39. Malachi

The New Testament Books

40. Matthew
Mark
Luke
43. John

Books of History

44. Acts

Epistles of Paul (Letters)

45. Romans.
46. Corinthians I
47. Corinthians II
48. Galatians
49. Ephesians
50. Philippians
51. Colossians
52. Thessalonians I
53. Thessalonians II
54. Timothy I
55. Timothy II

Books of Biography

56. Titus
57 Philemon
58. Hebrew

General Epistles (Letter

59. James
60. Peter I
61. Peter II
62. John I
63. John II)
64. John III
65. Jude

Books of Prophecy

66. Revelation

APPENDIX II

BREAK-DOWN OF THE CONTENT OF ISLAMIC LAW 1BADAT (Spiritual laws relating to the principles and acts of worship)

1. Tauhid (Unity of God)
2. Salat (Prayers)
3. Zakat (Obligatory aid to the poor)
4. Sawm (Fasting)
5. Hajj (Pilgrimage to the Holy Land)

AHWALUL SHASIYYA (Family Law)
1. Al-Zawaji (Marriage)
2. Talaq (Divorce)
3. Hadamah (Custody of Children)
4. Paternity
5. Waliyi (Guardianship)
6. Wasiyyah, Murath (Succession, Will)
7. Waqf (Pious Endowments)
8. Al-Hibah (Gift)

MU'AMALAT (Business transactions)
1. Moveable and Immovable Property
2. Mulk (Ownership)
3. Hanzu (Possession)
4. Aqdu (Contract)
5. Bai'u (Sale)
6. Ijarah (Hire)
7. Al-Rahn (Pledge, Trust and Mortgage)
8. Mudarabah (Partnership)
9. Shufu'a (Pre-emption)

UQUBAT (Criminal law)

1. Jinaya (Crimes)
2. Hadd (Punishments)
3. Qisas (Retaliation)
4. Jinayat (Torts)

AHKAM SULTANIYYAH (Laws of State)

1. Contempt
2. Sovereignty
3. Islamic State
4. Institution of Leadership
5. Doctrine of Power
6. Rule of Law
7. Citizenship
8. Fundamental Human Rights
9. Administrative Law

Machinery of Justice

1. Mahkamat (Courts)
2. Procedural Law
3. Shahala (Law of Evidence)
4. Muhtasib (Ombudsman)

SIYAR (International Law)

1. Private International Law
2. Public International Law
3. Jihad (The Law of War)
4. The Law of Neutrality

AKHLAQ (Moral Laws)

1. Nafsur (Self)
2. Ahalun (Family)

3. Jarutu (Neighbours)
4. Hayawanat (Animals)

APPENDIX III

*TABLE OF ORDINANCES AND DECREES, ETC AS THEY AFFECT ISLAMIC LAW IN NIGERIA BEFORE INDEPENDENCE**

1	Children and Young Persons Ordinance of 1943 (p.177)	Cap 31
2	Criminal Code Ordinance of 1916 (pp. 177-222)	Cap 42
3	Crown Lands Ordinance of 1918 (p. 179)	Cap 45
4	Interpretation Ordinance of 1939 (p 177)	Cap 94
5	Land and Native Rights Ordinance of 1916 (pp.179-189)	Cap 105
6	Land (Perpetual Succession) Ordinance of 1924 (p. 1 80)	Cap 107
7	Magistrate Courts Ordinance of 1943 (pp. 173-208)	Cap 122
8	Marriage Ordinance of 1914 (p. 178)	Cap 128
9	Native Children (Custody and Reformation) Ordinance of 1917 (p. 177)	Cap 141
10	Native Courts (Amendment Ordinance of 1951 (p. 183) No.2	Cap 1951
11	Native Courts Ordinance of 1933 (pp. 173-208)	Cap 142
12	Native Lands Acquisition Ordinance of 1917 (p. 180	Cap 144
13	Oaths and Affirmations Ordinance of 1942 (p. 180	Cap 162
14	Sheriffs and Enforcement of judgments and Orders Ordinance of 1945 (p. 171)	Cap 205
15	Slavery Ordinance of 1916 (pp. 178-2 15)	Cap 207
16	Supreme Court Ordinance of 1943 (pp. 173-208)	Cap 217

APPENDIX IV

*CHRONOLOGICAL ORDER OF EVENTS AFFECTING THE DEVELOPMENT OF THE SHARIA SYSTEM IN NIGERIA SINCE INDEPENDENCE**

30/9/60 (a) Sharia Court of Appeal Law came into force under the 1960 Constitution - powers were limited to Muslim Personal Law. Keay and Richardson opined that the Sharia Court of Appeal was raised to the level of High Courts in order to assure Muslims that Islamic law was recognized. Its decision was final.

1/10/60 (b) Provincial Courts were established in the Northern Region (Grade A, A limited and appellate jurisdiction over Grades B, C and D Native Courts).

(c) As a compromise, the Penal Code replaced Islamic Criminal Law in the North. It was said to be more suitable because it operated in India, Pakistan, Ceylon (Sirilanka), Libya and Sudan.

1963 (a) High Court Law of 1963, Section 62(i) provides for the constitution of the Court consisting of 3 judges (two of whom must be High Court judges while the third must be a judge of the Sharia Court of Appeal). This law was challenged in the Kano High Court (Ado, Hajiya Rabi Vs Hajiya Dija).

(b) At the first sitting of the High Court of Northern Nigeria (to hear an appeal filed by 1. S. Olawoyin) Chief Rotimi Williams, counsel for the plaintiff, pointed out that Section 59 of the High Court Law which provided for the inclusion of a Sharia Court Appeal judge was inconsistent with the Nigerian Constitution.

1966 (a) Major Chukwuma Nzeogwu, in his 4 day capacity as Administrator of the North, ordered the closure of all Native Courts in the North and the transfer of their cases to Magistrate Courts with immediate effect. Practical difficulties made the implementation of the directives impossible (there was only one Magistrate Court in Jos exercising jurisdiction over Plateau, Adaniawa, Bauchi and Borno Provinces and in Borno alone there were 50 Native Courts). The Nzeogwu directives have to be suspended because they would have resulted in chaos.

(b) Major-General Aguiyi Ironsi set up a Study Group on Judicial Services to look into the administration of justice in the North.

(c) Major Hassan Usman Katsina, in his capacity as Governor of the Northern Region, was directed to abolish all Emir's Courts in the Region.

1968 Area Courts Edict enacted to replace Native Courts Law of 1956.

1972 All Nigeria Judges Conference held in Lagos recommended the establishment of a Federal Sharia Court of Appeal. The court when established is to handle all appeals in Islamic Law coming from the States (details to be found in a paper written by Justice A. N. Aniagolu).

1976 (a) General Murtala Muhammed appointed an Area Courts Reform Committee of eminent judges and a Grand Qadi to determine the need for continuity or otherwise of the Area Courts system.

(b) General Olusegun Obasanjo received the report of the Committee on the 23rd of July 1976. The Committee recommended the retention of the Area Courts because of their relevance at grassroots level to speedy administration of justice (reported to handle about 95% of all cases). It suggested the appointment of a Grand Mufti and 3 Muftis as judges of the Court.

1978 (a) Constitution Drafting Committee appointed by General M. Mohammed and chaired by Chief Rotimi Williams submitted its report to General O. Obasanjo. The Committee recommended the establishment of a Federal Sharia Court of Appeal as a matter of necessity.

(b) The Constituent Assembly passed a resolution rejecting the establishment of a Federal Sharia Court of Appeal. It went further to make provisions curtailing the jurisdiction of State Court of Appeal. General Obasanjo had to intervene to abate the heated debate on the issue.

1980 The future of Islamic Courts was raised at the Sixth Commonwealth Law Conference held in 1980. The issue was left in abeyance at the request of a representative with a remark that the Courts would be phased out gradually with time.

1985 The Hon. Justice Obi Okoye, Chief Judge of Plateau State, ordered the removal of all criminal jurisdiction from the Plateau State Area Courts and transferred them to Magistrate Courts. His only authority was that the then retiring Chief Justice of the Federation who was on a farewell tour of the States casually remarked that the time has come when criminal jurisdiction should be removed from the Area Courts. This decision was reversed when it was discovered that prisons in Plateau State were over congested with detainees awaiting trial.

1986 General Ibrahim Babangida signed Decree No. 26, The Constitution (Suspension and Modification) (Amendment) to correct an anomaly in the Constitution which allowed Christian judges to sit and hear appeals from Islamic Courts.

1987 General Ibrahim Babangida inaugurated the Constitution Review Committee on the 7th of September 1987 and charged it with the responsibility of reviewing the 1879 Constitution as part of the preparatory work of the Armed Forces Ruling Council to return Nigeria to a democratically- elected civilian administration by the year 1992.

1988 (a) The Constitution Review Committee completed its work on the 12th of February 1989 and submitted its reports to

President Ibrahim Babangida. The Committee, among other things, recommended the retention of Sharia at State and the Federal Capital but remained silent on the idea of establishing a Federal Shana Court of Appeal.

(b) General Ibrahim Babangida inaugurated the second Constituent Assembly on the 11th of May 1988 to deliberate on the provisions of the Draft Constitution and to make appropriate recommendations to the Federal Government. While presenting its report to the President, the Chairman, Justice A. N. Aniagolu observed that by far the most problematic, in terms of emotional impact and potential dangers, of all the issues the Assembly handled, was that of the Sharia. Some members of the Assembly indicated their intention to recommend again the adoption of a Federal Sharia Court of Appeal in the new Constitution and those who were opposed to the idea took an extreme stand on the issue by insisting that Sharia be expunged altogether from the Constitution. In order to avert the obvious danger that could result if the debate was allowed, the Government removed from the jurisdiction of the Assembly clauses 6(2) to 6(6(d) and 248 to 263 which deal with the subject.

APPENDIX V

On the Concept of Compassion ·

Is compassion central to Islam? Many people think *jihad* is more central to it than compassion. At least this is the general impression of people including of course Muslims. But this is not so. Compassion is far more central to Islam than *jihad*. It is certain happenings in history of Islam and also in contemporary world that this impression about *jihad* goes round.

In fact compassion represents the true spirit of Islam and compassion is far more vital to Islamic teachings than any thing else. In fact compassion in Islam, after the concepts of unity of God (*tawhid*) and the messengership of Muhammad, *risalah*, is as central to Islam as it is to Buddhism. We will throw light on compassion in Islam in the following pages.

There are certain key words in the Qur'an which are greatly stressed of which four are very often repeated i.e. *rahmah, ihsan 'adl*, and *hikmah* (compassion, benevolence, justice and wisdom). *Rahmah* (compassion, mercy) and its roots abound in the Holy Qur'an. Among Allah's own names are *Rahman* and *Rahim* (compassionate and Merciful). A Muslim begins everything by reciting *Bi Ism-i- Allah al-Rahman al-Rahim* (i.e. begin in the name of Allah Who is Compassionate and Merciful). Thus a Muslim is supposed to invoke Allah the Compassionate and Merciful at every step. He does not invoke Allah 's other names (Allah has 99 names according to the Islamic belief) as he invokes Him as Merciful and Compassionate.

The very first chapter of the Qur'an has the second verse as *Al-Rehman al-Rahim* (The Compassionate, the Merciful). The first verse too carries the sense of compassion when it describes Allah as *Rabb al-'Alamin* (i.e. Sustainer of the whole world). The concept of sustenance of the whole world itself is based on His Mercy and Compassion for every thing He has created. In fact rahmah is so central to Allah's existence that it embraces all that exists in the universe (wasi`at kulla shayin) see verse 40:7.

In fact He sent His Messenger Muhammad also as the Mercy of the World (21:107). Thus the Prophet of Islam also represents universal mercy. As the Messenger of Allah he is representative of His Mercy and hence the Prophet himself is known as *rahmatan lil `alamin* (mercy of the worlds). Thus a true follower of the Prophet (PBUH) has to be merciful and compassionate to the extent humanly possible. Any one who is cruel and has no sensitivity towards sufferings of others cannot be Prophet's true follower in any sense.

This is a great pity that Muslims themselves except the sufis and their followers have forgotten the emphasis of the Holy Qur'an on the quality of compassion. The Sufis lay tremendous stress on compassion. Their very fundamental doctrine is what is called *sulh-i-kul*, i.e. peace with all which means no violence and no aggressiveness. The majority of Muslims of course follow sufi approach. It is only some frustrated fringe groups of Muslims who keep on talking of *jihad* and power.

It is important to note that in Qur'an there is no concept of war of aggression and no concept of permissiveness of violence. Even where permission of war has been given it has been given to defend and protect rights of the oppressed and exploited, and not for achieving power. There is no verse in the Qur'an which permits violence for conquering territory or for achieving power. In fact war has been qualified in the Qur'an by the words *fi' sabilillah*, i.e. in the way of Allah. Thus a war can be fought, if at all necessary, not for any personal ambitions or for grabbing territory or not for personal animosity or for revenge but only in the way of Allah.

And what is the way of Allah? Allah's way is of justice, Allah's way is of protecting the rights of the poor and exploited. In fact, the very first verse in the Qur'an permitting the use of violence reflects this very well. It says:

> "And what reason you have not to fight in the way of Allah, and of the weak among the men and the women and the children, who say: Our Lord, take us out of this town, whose people are oppressors, and grant us from Thee a friend, and grant us from Thee a helper." (4:75) (emphasis added).

Thus explaining the import of this verse, a noted commentator, Maulana Muhammad Ali, says in his The Holy Qur'an (Lahore, 1973, pp-211)

> " This verse explains what is meant by fighting in the way of Allah. While most of the believers who had the means had escaped from Makkah, which is here spoken of as the city whose people are oppressors, there remained those who were weak and unable to undertake a journey. These were still persecuted and oppressed by the Makkans, as is clearly shown by the words of the verse, and not only men, but even women and young children, were persecuted. Fighting to deliver them from the persecution of the oppressors was really fighting in the way of Allah. ..."

Since any fighting has been permitted only in the way of Allah it cannot be a war of aggression in any case. It has to be only on compassionate grounds, not on any ground and hence the doctrine of compassion remains central. If there is no other way to liberate the oppressed except through use of force, only then will the use of force be justified; otherwise not.

The Qur'an, again and again, shows its sympathy for the weaker sections of the society in which it includes, among others, the orphans, the widows, the poor and the exploited, the slaves and other politically or socially and economically oppressed people. It emphasises different ways of helping them. This is all on the grounds of compassion. Compassion really means sensitivity to the suffering of others. A person cannot be compassionate unless he/she is sensitive to others' suffering. And this suffering includes, as we will show, not only human beings but also animals and plants.

First, let us take the suffering of human beings. The Qur'an shows great compassion to orphans, the widows, the poor and the slaves. It wants to liberate these poorer and oppressed sections from their situation. *Zakah*, a toll tax, has been made obligatory on all believing Muslims, men or women to help these sections. Thus the Qur'an says,

> "Zakat, charity is only for the poor and the needy and those employed to administer it, and those whose hearts are made to incline, and (to free) the captives, and those in debt, and in the way of Allah and for the wayfarer - an ordinance from Allah. And Allah is Knowing, Wise." (9:60)

Thus all the categories indicated in the above verse except two, i.e. those who administer it (i.e. collect the zakah on behalf of the Islamic state or *bayt al-mal* (state treasury) and 'those whose hearts are to be inclined or won over (by Muslims for their help) all other categories are of weaker sections of society - those who suffer, i.e. the poor, the needy, the captives (in war), those indebted (who but the poor are indebted), the slaves and the wayfarers. They all stand in need of help. A believer who is well off must be sensitive to the needs of these categories and must help them financially to remove their sufferings on compassionate grounds. Thus even for the payment of *zakat* compassion remains central.

Not only that the Qur'an wants to remove those who are arrogant because of their wealth and power and empower the weak so that there is no suffering in the world. It says clearly and unambiguously "And We desired to bestow a favour upon those who were deemed weak in the land, and to make them the leaders, and to make them the inheritors." (28:5) Thus the Qur'an favours the mustad`ifin (the weaker sections) to the mustakbirin (those powerful and arrogant).

www.ingramcontent.com/pod-product-compliance
Lightning Source LLC
Chambersburg PA
CBHW022105240926
51848CB00008B/150
* 9 7 8 9 7 8 1 5 6 5 1 4 4 *